SELLING
OR
BUYING
A
MEDICAL
PRACTICE

SELLING
OR
BUYING
A
MEDICAL
PRACTICE

GARY R. SCHAUB, MBA

MEDICAL ECONOMICS BOOKS
ORADELL, NEW JERSEY 07649

Library of Congress Cataloging-in-Publication Data

Schaub, Gary R.
    Selling or buying a medical practice/Gary R. Schaub.
    ISBN 0-87489-487-5
    1. Medicine—Practice—Economic aspects.   I. Title.
    [DNLM: 1. Practice Management, Medical—economics.   W 80
  S313s]
    R728.S415 1988
  610'.68'1—dc19
  DNLM/DLC
  for Library of Congress   88-13307
                                                                                    CIP

ISBN 0-87489-487-5

Medical Economics Company Inc.
Oradell, New Jersey 07649

Printed in the United States of America

CONTENTS

CHAPTER 3 **PRACTICE VALUATION** 41

CHAPTER 4 **GROUPS, PARTNERSHIPS, CLINICS & CORPORATIONS** 67

CHAPTER 5 **MAXIMIZING PRACTICE VALUATION** 75

CHAPTER 6 **FINDING THE RIGHT BUYER OR ASSOCIATE**   105

CHAPTER 7 **NEGOTIATING SUCCESSFULLY**   119

ix

SELLING
OR
BUYING
A
MEDICAL
PRACTICE

1

THE BEGINNING OF THE END

"Dr. Older is no longer in practice and has stopped seeing patients. If you need a doctor, please call the medical staff department at the hospital. This is a recording…"

One Monday morning, Dr. Older's patients were greeted with this recording. He had decided to shut down his practice. Patients calling the hospital were given the names of other physicians in the community where the patients could transfer their care. Apparently, this physician had decided to retire and had simply closed his doors.

Contrast that scenario to Dr. Wiser, a client who recently retired. His practice was growing, was in a good location, and had an excellent staff. The buyer was a recent graduate. Dr. Wiser received a cash down payment of $35,000, a monthly check for $1,785 for the next sixty months, plus about $50,000 in accounts receivable that were collected over a three- to four-month time period.

Both practices were in the same city and both doctors retired at about the same time. Obviously, their names have been changed for this story, but the facts are true. They could be physicians, dentists, physical therapists; they could be in solo practice, group practice, or incorpo-

1

rated. The difference is that one retiring doctor planned ahead, got expert advice and assistance, and now is enjoying his retirement. The other doctor, Dr. Older, let his practice dwindle and simply closed his doors. Lack of planning and knowledge about the value of a health care practice probably cost that doctor over $100,000. This could have been a significant portion of his retirement finances.

Based on the author's experience with over $25,000,000 worth of practices, the average medical practice has the following value, as shown in Figure 1. This value does not include any facility which the doctor also may own.

Figure 1
MEDICAL PRACTICE VALUE

Goodwill	$80,000
Furniture/Equipment/Supplies	$34,000
Accounts Receivable	$45,000
TOTAL	$159,000

The purpose of this book is to explore the reasons practices have value, how to determine this value, and how to receive this value from a qualified buyer. The book is mainly written from the seller's perspective, but includes specific areas that potential buyers will find helpful in their quest for practices. The more knowledge that both sellers and buyers have about this process enhances the successful transfers of practices at fair values.

During talks and seminars about this subject, I notice that after showing the average value figures for practices, the audiences become very animated, start taking copious notes, and fix their attention on what I am saying. Doctors who are contemplating retirement or a practice change begin to get smiles on their faces. Younger colleagues, thinking of going into private practice, begin to turn a little green around the gills and look like something just gave them Salmonella poisoning. After finishing this book you will understand where these values come from and why buying a practice is the best investment that a new physician can make.

When thinking about selling your practice, look upon it as an opportunity, not a problem. You have the opportunity to continue excellent clinical care for your patients. The buyer has the opportunity to grow in an established practice. The result will be more financial security for both the buyer and the seller.

This book is written for all health care providers, including physicians, dentists and physical therapists. The basics are the same, no matter the type of practice. Specific examples will be given to explain a concept that applies to all professional categories. The bottom line is the continuance of excellent clinical care for patients, whether this is in the field of medicine, physical therapy or oral health.

WHY DO PRACTICES HAVE VALUE?

The answer to this question is obvious. The number of doctors has grown much more quickly than the population in recent years. Any health care magazine, newspaper or newsletter concerning practice management will have several articles concerning this topic. According to the AMA Center for Health Policy Research, the number of medical school graduates has increased from 8,974 in 1970–71 to 16,191 in 1985–86 (*The Demographics of Physician Supply: Trends and Projections*—1987). This is an 80.4% increase in the size of graduating classes.

This large growth in the number of medical school graduates has not spread evenly among all specialties. Figure 2 shows the differences in growth by specialty group. Between 1980 and 1985, anesthesiology grew faster than all other specialties. This was followed by internal medicine and pediatrics.

The physician-to-population ratio recently has shown a corresponding increase. From 1930 to 1960, the ratio ranged between 125 and 140 physicians per 100,000 population. However, during the early 1960s this ratio slowly began to rise. From the 1970s until now this ratio skyrocketed as government programs encouraged physician supply and more college graduates became interested in health care careers. Figure 3 documents this trend.

This would not be a problem if patient utilization of medical services also increased during this time frame. However, according to the same source, the average patient visits per week among non-federal patient care physicians declined from 130.8 per week in 1982 to 118.0 in 1986. This is a statistically significant decrease of 9.8%.

These trends also are happening in the dental field. For example, in Nebraska the number of licensed dentists has increased 3.7 times faster than the population of Nebraska during the past ten years (*Nebraska Dental Manpower Study*—1987).

You do not need dry statistics to indicate what is happening daily in your practices. Most of you have added, or are thinking of adding, a new word to your practice management vocabulary—marketing. The purpose of marketing is to add new patient growth to practices. This is a direct impact of these statistics.

Figure 2

PERCENT GROWTH IN ACTIVE PHYSICIAN
POPULATION BY SPECIALTY, 1980-85

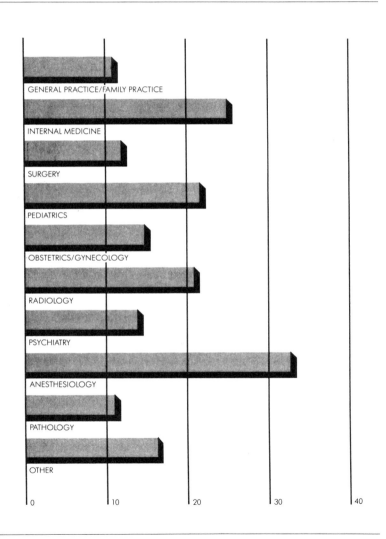

SOURCE: 1980-85 AMA Physician Masterfile.

Figure 3

ACTIVE PHYSICIANS PER 100,000 U.S.
POPULATION, 1900 TO 1985

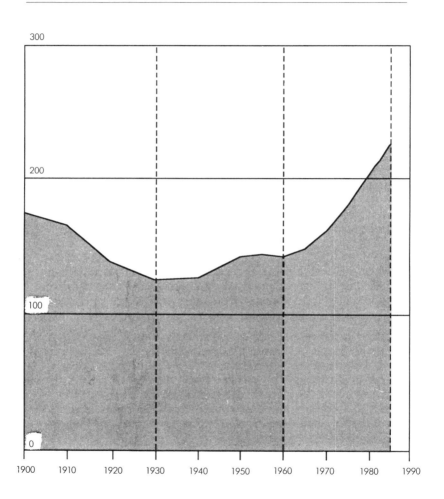

SOURCE: 1950-85 AMA Physician Masterfile
1900-45 Historical Statistics of the U.S., Colonial times to 1970

At this point you may be wondering why this state of affairs would have a positive impact on practice value. The answer is that all of these new graduates have limited options in terms of going into private practice. In the past, hanging out a shingle and then closing the practice to new patients a few months or years later was all that was necessary to be successful. This is not true today. For example, in Oregon during the past two years only four dentists have started practices from scratch. What have the other one hundred plus new graduates done? Most of them have purchased existing practices.

WHY ARE PRACTICES BEING PURCHASED?

The law of supply and demand is shifting. More professional practices are being purchased. Just a few years ago, practice sales did not normally occur. Why are there buyers now willing to purchase a practice? The basic answer is patient flow. Buyers are willing to purchase a practice in order to assume an active patient appointment book. An existing practice has more value to them than does the alternative of finding, equipping and setting up a practice from scratch.

The following examples may shed more light on this:

New Graduates: Purchasing an existing practice is the best and sometimes the only way for a new professional to start in private practice.

Competition: Colleagues are looking for less competition for patients by merging practices. Solo physicians are becoming absorbed by groups; medical groups are becoming absorbed by hospitals; and larger clinics are becoming more group-oriented. Larger practices believe they are

better able to cope with the changing demands of the
health care field.

Expansion of Practices: Some doctors are being caught
in a low production/high fixed expense practice. The only
way they can grow is to buy other practices and increase
their production and net income. Other professionals want
to do more management aspects of practice and have
associates take over the actual clinical care. This requires
more patients in order to succeed.

Satellite Practices: These are becoming more prevalent
as health care providers try to find patients for their
practices. A satellite practice enables a practice to grow
with a community. The best way to do this is to buy out an
existing practice in the area to establish a presence.

Relocation: Many doctors relocate because of spouse
career changes or quality of life changes. Thus, purchasing
a practice is the best way to quickly become established in
a new location.

It can cost up to $100,000 to start a practice from
scratch. The beginning practice will have losses at first, the
doctor will need personal living expenses until the new
practice reaches a break-even level, and then, hopefully,
will have a reasonable personal income. However, the
initial $100,000 still has to be paid back to the financing
sources.

On the other hand, a doctor purchasing a practice
should, over a five-year period, be able to pay off the
practice purchase price, receive a reasonable personal
living income, and then receive all of the practice net
income as personal income. The alternative—starting a
new practice—will cost just as much but will be a more

risky business proposition. Buying an existing practice minimizes this risk level.

In summary, a buyer wants an on going practice for the following reasons:

- The practice has a track record. It has a past history of collections, expenses and net income. It should be relatively safe to predict what the practice will do for the buyer in the future. With a scratch practice, collections and net income are only a calculated guess.

- The practice is probably beyond the break-even point. It will make money for the buyer the day he or she purchases the practice. With a start-up practice, sizable losses will occur before a net income is created.

- The practice is free of start-up problems. It has patients, referral sources, employees, suppliers, and a physical plant and equipment in operation.

- The practice should be available for less than it would cost to duplicate the assets with a scratch practice.

Buyers may be able to justify starting a new practice, and not purchasing an existing one, in two specific situations. The first is if the new doctor has a unique practice format in mind. An existing practice may not have the necessary equipment, patient demographics, or practice profile to fit the new format. In this case it does not make sense to pay for equipment or goodwill that will not be used in the new practice. The second reason is location. If an excellent new location is available, then it may outweigh the advantages of purchasing a practice that is not in that particular location. These are the only two situations where a start-up practice might make sense. However, these two situations do not occur very frequently.

Before leaving this section, a critical point needs to be emphasized. It will be discussed many times in later chapters. The only reason it makes sense to sell a practice or to purchase a practice is for the patient flow. Ongoing, transferable patient flow is the basic reason that practices have value. Many buyers lose sight of this objective when examining various practices or negotiating for the purchase of a specific practice. When negotiations get bogged down over the value of a box of syringes, both buyer and seller have lost sight of the final objective. Unless both parties keep this fact uppermost in their minds, the successful transfer of the practice will be in question.

WHAT ARE THE REASONS FOR SELLING A PRACTICE?

Based upon experience with about one hundred fifty practices, the major reasons for selling are as follows:

- Retirement
- Disability
- Merger with a partner or group
- Career change
- Relocation
- Leaving private practice to join a government agency, health maintenance organization, armed forces, or other health care provider
- Returning for more education

The decision to sell usually is very difficult to make. The first problem generally is one of a lack of knowledge.

Most professionals do not sell their practices more than once in their careers, so it is difficult to build up expertise in this area. However, once the process is explained, most doctors are surprised at how easy the process can be, if valid assumptions are used and experts are consulted during the various phases of the selling process.

The emotional aspect of the decision, as is true for most major personal decisions, is the most difficult part. Besides the mechanics of the sale process itself, other factors come into play. These factors can be how to proceed into a satisfactory retirement, cope with a disability, make a career change, or other major emotional considerations. Because of the seriousness of this part of the sale process, Chapter Two will address this specifically.

With many clients, once the decision to sell the practice has been made after consultation, they immediately want to sell. They probably have worried, stewed, contorted and panicked many times, but once the information is at hand, they proceed at once on the chosen path. For example, after completing an appraisal and discussing the results with the doctor, I will get a telephone call in about one week stating that instead of waiting for a year or two they want to sell *yesterday*. Priorities seem to change very quickly. All of this is simply the important part that knowledge can play in any emotionally-oriented decision.

When should this process start? I recommend that any professional thinking of selling a practice should try to plan at least two years in advance. This usually can occur with a long-range retirement plan or merger. However, many instances preclude the luxury of long-term planning. Sudden disability, spouse employment change, divorce, or other act can move the sale date up drastically. In these cases the sale still can proceed, but may be limited in attaining optimal value. This also will be discussed in more detail in the final chapters of the book.

WHAT ARE SOME REASONS FOR HAVING AN APPRAISAL DONE?

In order to value a practice, an appraisal needs to be completed. Obviously, if the practice is to be sold in the near future, an appraisal is the first step in the sale process. However, in my experience, about three appraisals are done for every practice that is sold. The following are some of the more common reasons for having just an appraisal done:

- Establishing a value when adding an associate or partner
- Planning ahead for retirement, estate valuation, or personal financial planning
- Divorce proceeding
- Dividing up a group practice or partnership
- Financing arrangements
- Insurance coverage

If you are reading this book only to understand the process of having your practice appraised, then pay particular attention to the chapters on valuation techniques, the appraisal, and maximizing practice value. In any case, it is important to understand what an appraisal is about and to insure that the appraisal is done in a qualified manner. You need to understand the elements that affect the value of *your* practice. Even if an appraisal is the only need at this time, in the future your practice probably will be sold. The knowledge gained now can help to maximize future practice valuation and to minimize the emotional stress that results from a practice sale.

WHY SHOULD I BUY A PRACTICE?

This is the first question that is asked when lecturing to students. In the universal wisdom of youth, they also answer the question before I can respond. I have been told the following:

> "You should not buy a practice, because you will lose forty percent of the patients."

> "It is not worth it to go into more debt."

> "I will not have any problem attracting patients to my new practice."

> "There is no such thing as goodwill. How can a doctor ask money for his patients?"

Since these answers to the above question are all false, why do many students and newly graduated doctors believe that they are true? Again, this probably is caused by a lack of knowledge about the practice sale process. This lack of knowledge is created by the minimal training that most health care students are given concerning practice management. In addition, many instructors and professors may have chosen an academic career pathway because they did not like, or could not succeed, in private practice. Schools themselves seem to minimize the potentially critical practice management decisions facing physicians and dentists in today's health care environment. The chancellor of a leading medical school once told me that he never would allow practice management courses to be given to residents, because the school was dedicated to turning out physicians who only cared for the humanistic aspects of medicine. Somehow the business aspects of practice must be considered inhuman, according to the thought process of this particular educator. Hopefully, this practice management awareness will be taught in the schools.

Recent graduates have various career pathways open to them after medical or dental schooling is complete. A partial list is as follows:

- Armed forces
- Health maintenance organizations
- Government agencies, such as public health
- Hospitals
- Academia
- Private practice

If the student chooses the private practice pathway, the decision has to be made whether to buy an existing practice, to buy into a group, to start from scratch, or to become an associate or an employee. In my experience, joining the Armed Forces or a government health care agency is a good way to make the transition from eight to twelve years of undergraduate and postgraduate education to living and working in the "real world." After one to three years of this experience, the decision as to how to proceed to private practice is usually easier to make and is based upon a more realistic appraisal of the pluses and minuses of this career pathway.

Practicing doctors also may find that the easiest way to expand their existing practices is to purchase another practice. One client sold his practice to a younger colleague down the hall in his building. The patients followed the staff to the new location and new doctor. The equipment was donated to a voluntary health care clinic for the homeless. The transition was very successful for everyone—including the patients, staff, retiring doctor, and the buyer. One doctor bought a small practice from the estate of a deceased colleague, and six months later doubled the size of her practice by purchasing another estate situation. She was able to make the second purchase quickly, and successfully integrated the patients because of the experience gained the first time.

It is just as important for the buyer to make a practice purchase decision based upon knowledge and planning as it is for the seller. In many instances I will perform an appraisal for a buyer who is interested in purchasing a practice. This is similar to getting a second opinion for surgery. The cost of the appraisal is minor compared to the value of the increased knowledge gained about the proposed transaction.

PLANNING, PLANNING, PLANNING.

The importance of planning, in terms of a successful practice sale or purchase, is similar to the three basic rules of real estate investing. The three rules are: 1) location; 2) location; and 3) location. Planning will insure that when it comes time to sell your practice, a buyer will be found to purchase it. Planning ahead will enable you to maximize your personal and financial goals from the practice sale.

It is critical to keep the practice at its peak, rather than let it deteriorate. Improvements are made on a house or commercial property in order to improve resale value. Do the same for your practice to maximize its value. It is a good idea to begin planning at least two years in advance, especially for some of the subspecialty practices. Subspecialists are more limited in number, and many make practice location decisions early in their careers before completing schooling.

WHAT ABOUT CONFIDENTIALITY?

Confidentiality is a critical issue when appraising or selling a practice. Once a "For Sale" sign is put in front of your practice, the damage is done. Word travels fast. Patients and staff members get upset and nervous if they think that you are leaving the practice. Patients are concerned about who the new person may be, what his or her background is, and the loss of the rapport and support that have been the basis for their doctor/patient relationship. Staff members obviously are concerned about their future employment status. For these reasons it is critical that confidentiality be maintained until your plans are firm.

An innocent appraisal, for whatever reason, can be misconstrued. Therefore, if you are getting an appraisal for reasons other than selling the practice, it is wise to tell the staff why the appraisal is being done. This will help to minimize the staff's apprehensions. A professional appraiser can accomplish the appraisal in a confidential manner. Find out how this can be done before proceeding.

One client, in a small city, did not want word of his practice sale to leak out before it was accomplished. He was a pillar of the community, involved in many community activities, and knew that he would be swamped with inquiries if anyone found out about his plans. We were able to transfer the practice successfully. No one knew of the change until the Monday morning that the new doctor walked into the practice.

Unfortunately, in another instance, the selling physician was accosted in the doctors' lounge of the community hospital by a colleague, who loudly informed everyone that the physician was getting ready to sell his practice. The source of the leak was a candidate who also had interviewed with another group in the same city. Even though the candidate had been told to keep the practice sale confidential, he had not done so. Luckily, the practice was sold quickly to another candidate, so the damage to the selling doctor's referral sources was minimized.

Maintaining too much confidentiality can have negative drawbacks also. It makes the practice more difficult to sell. The more people who are aware of the potential availability of a practice, the easier and quicker a buyer can be found. Thus, the need for confidentiality needs to be balanced with the need for the timing of the sale. Confidentiality is not such a big problem with general practices, because patients probably will not find out about the sale ahead of time. However, for subspecialty practices dependent upon other doctors' referrals, the damage can be greater because the referral sources may cut back on referring new patients, since the future of the practice is in doubt.

WHAT ARE THE ELEMENTS OF A SUCCESSFUL SALE?

For a successful practice sale, you need patients. Patients are the end product of your entire business enterprise. Patient flow is the reason someone will buy the practice or come in as an associate. A new buyer can step into the practice with an ongoing patient load. This is why he or she wants to purchase the practice—to get a head start on the future. Therefore, the first element of a successful sale is *active patients*.

Many doctors have stopped accepting new patients, have referred younger patients out, and have taken other steps to limit their practice growth. If at all possible, avoid doing this. New patient growth is the lifeblood of the practice and enhances its value.

Keeping patients active is also important. Maintain a recall system if you are in general practice. The more active patients that you have, again, the higher the value of your practice.

For better or worse, people categorize other people into stereotypes based upon first impressions. People make judgments about others within the first four minutes of contact. Therefore, first impressions must be positive. If the initial impression of your practice by a potential buyer or a new patient is negative, even your best clinical or personal skills may not be able to overcome this negative impression. Try to see the practice objectively through the buyer's eyes.

Practice net income is the major determinant of practice value. A higher net income available, as a percentage of collections, will increase the amount of money available to a buyer to pay for the practice. Try to decrease overhead, if you have a high overhead practice. This will not only increase the value of the practice, and your own net income before the sale, but an efficient practice generally is also more fun to be involved with. The concepts concerning maximizing practice value will be developed further in Chapter Five. They are a very important part of the overall strategy for selling.

To obtain the best results in a practice sale, it is necessary to consult an array of advisers. Since selling the practice will be one of your biggest life decisions, the more help you can get, the better the results. Advisers can assist as follows:

Practice Consultant or Broker

- Reduces the amount of your time spent in the process
- Locates and screens potential buyers
- Indicates ways to increase practice value
- Facilitates third party negotiations
- Assists in locating financing for the buy-out

Attorney and CPA

- Informs you of tax ramifications of sale
- Advises and draws up legal contracts

Banker

- Helps with credit screening of candidates
- Assists with financial arrangements

Colleagues

- Talk with colleagues who have gone through the process of selling their practices. They can be a good source of ideas and warn of problem areas. However, be very careful to separate the wheat from the chaff, as colleagues sometimes have difficulty being frank about problems or financial results.

Societies

- Organized health care societies, such as local component, state, and national medical and dental societies, are excellent sources of background information and potential buyers.

Using advisers is very important. Many practice sales can become practice sale fiascos. This seldom occurs if the seller utilizes some or all of the above resources. When a large amount of money and the future is at stake, doctor-to-doctor negotiations almost invariably lead to disaster. You are good at providing clinical care. However, you usually refer patients whose problems are not part of your specialty or training. Do the same with the practice sale. The results will invariably be better than if you did the entire process yourself. These advisers are worth the fees they charge, since the practice sale price may be greater, and the likelihood of failure may be much less.

Overall, the practice sale strategy will depend on the individual situation. Long-term planning gives a chance to enhance practice value, to check out resources more thoroughly, and to be more selective about potential buyers. Shorter term considerations, such as disability or relocation, alter this and decrease options and negotiating leverage. Whatever route you choose to follow, the guidelines in this book will pay off handsomely on the bottom line—both financially and emotionally.

WHAT ARE THE SUCCESSFUL ELEMENTS OF A PRACTICE PURCHASE?

As a buyer evaluating practices to purchase, the following questions need to be answered:

- Can you find the practice?
- Can you make an earning from the practice?
- Can you manage the practice?
- Can you enjoy the practice?
- Can you afford the practice?

Selecting the right practice to purchase is not just an economic decision, it is also a personal decision. The practice should fit your proposed clinical style, the location where you want to live, and the future earnings potential that you want. Another important consideration, if the practice is a group, is the compatibility of the partners, both personal and clinical.

When looking at a practice, try to avoid common pitfalls. The most important consideration is the potential for patient or referral loss. Competition also needs to be evaluated. Are competitors moving into the area, setting up practices or clinics that would siphon patients from your practice? Is the neighborhood in a declining area, which means future patient loss? Can the lease on the office be assumed so that you will be able to stay in the location for a reasonable length of time?

The financial aspects of the purchase decision need to be tackled from two sides. Side one is the practice financial picture. Project what the collections and expenses for the practice will be based upon the way *you* plan to manage it. This pro forma economic analysis should be projected two to three years to get an accurate assessment of the practice's capabilities.

The second side is your personal financial picture. Most practice purchases require bank financing by the buyer to initiate the purchase. Most potential purchasers are still heavily in debt from school and have very few assets. The banks will look at personal character, cash flow, collateral, capital, and insurance coverage. There are many creative ways to handle the practice purchase, which will be discussed in a later chapter. In my experience, I have never had a practice sale not be consummated because the purchaser could not raise the money.

The critical phase of a practice purchase, after the financial part has been completed, is the actual transfer of the practice to the buyer. During this transfer several things need to be considered. Employee loyalty and enthusiasm need to be transferred to you; patients need to be transferred; more credit may need to be arranged; any changes must be made slowly; and the practice should be managed on a "lean and mean" concept until the financial picture is clear.

Advisers should be consulted. Consultants and practice brokers can assist in finding the right practice. Attorneys and CPAs need to be utilized to assist with the financial and legal aspects of the transfer. Colleagues who have recently purchased practices should be interviewed, and their advice given serious consideration. Your spouse is also a critical player in the purchase decision.

Planning is just as important for the buyer as for the seller. It can not eliminate all the unknowns from the process, but can certainly reduce the major risks that may be encountered.

WHAT ABOUT COVERING MY TAIL?

As a selling doctor, covering your tail is not writing a memo to protect yourself from future damages caused by a clinical problem or a personal problem. It has to do with malpractice insurance. Many doctors, especially sub-specialists, may find themselves ready to retire in a few years but will receive a bill for $100,000 or more from their malpractice carrier. This bill is for the retroactive reporting endorsement (commonly called the tail) for their claims-made malpractice insurance policy.

In the past, most doctors were covered on an occurrence basis. This meant that if you were covered by a policy on the *date* that an alleged malpractice act occurred, the policy would cover the claim up to the limits in effect as of that date. However, with the malpractice insurance crisis, virtually all carriers have changed to a claims-made policy. This means that you are covered for an alleged malpractice act if you had a claims-made policy in force on the date that the *claim* was filed, not the date the act occurred.

Claims-made insurance is less expensive than occur-rence insurance. During the first five years of the policy

Figure 4

CLAIMS MADE VS. OCCURRENCE
PREMIUMS

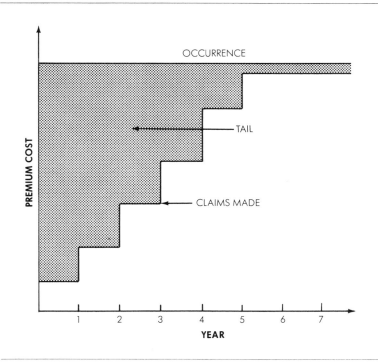

the premium is slowly stepped up to where it eventually is about the same as an occurrence policy. Figure 4 indicates this premium step rate function.

The underlined area in Figure 4 represents the percentage of the then in force premium which has not been paid. When retiring, or changing carriers, this retroactive premium amount needs to be paid. In addition, future coverage is needed in case a claim is made, after you have stopped practice, for an alleged act that occurred while you were practicing. The statute of limitations in many states usually limits this to five years from the date of the incident, or two years from the date of discovery of the problem.

What effect can this have on your practice? A surgeon client recently retired, and the down payment for his practice, $25,000, went directly to the insurance company to cover his tail. An OB/GYN client who wants to retire in five years now has a tail premium of $100,000, which will probably increase by the time of retirement. Thus, it is possible that your entire practice sale money will have to go to an insurance carrier, not to your retirement plan.

Claims-made insurance can be positive, as most doctors have increased their limits in the past few years. A claim made now will be covered based upon these higher limits. Under an occurrence policy, if you had $300,000 in coverage a few years ago when the act took place, that would have been the limit of the coverage, rather than $1,000,000 + which most doctors now carry.

What can be done about paying the tail coverage? Many state societies are lobbying for insurance companies to forgive this tail premium if the doctor has been insured with the carrier for a number of years. Some doctors may prefer to go bare, if they are in general practice, a non-surgical specialty, or in a community where malpractice claims are not often made. The statute of limitations also can be used to determine how much tail coverage should be purchased.

Since I have seen this problem occurring frequently in practice sales, I sometimes have advised clients to arrange for a special life insurance policy. This policy is taken out before retirement and the cash value is calculated to be equal to the amount of tail premium required when retirement is commenced. This cash value accumulates tax free and represents an inexpensive way to plan on paying this major expenditure. In addition, the pure insurance part of the policy will insure that your estate is not touched in paying the tail coverage at the time of your death. Buying the tail coverage at this time also insures that your estate will not be liable for any malpractice claims, up to your malpractice policy limits.

Figure 5

OLDER VERSUS WISER

	Dr. Older	Dr. Wiser
Practice Transfer	"I closed my practice."	"Dr. Eager has assumed my practice."
Financial		
Goodwill	None	$ 80,000
Equipment	Donation value	$ 35,000
Receivables	$ 20,000	$ 50,000
Total	$ 20,000+	$165,000
Future Plans	Collect Social Security.	Enjoy more travel.
		Aloha!

This is just another example of the complexities of practice today. However, good planning for the future can minimize the trauma and stress of these complexities.

As a conclusion to this chapter, I would like you to remember the examples given concerning Drs. Older and Wiser (Figure 5). Dr. Older let the goodwill and patient flow that he had built up over the years drop to zero. Dr. Wiser was able to retire in a more comfortable manner than he had previously planned. His new buyer is increasing the growth of the practice and enjoying the psychic and financial benefits of making a good practice buying decision. Would you rather be Older or Wiser? The choice is yours.

2
OVERCOMING EMOTIONAL BARRIERS

"It is romantic to want to die with
your boots on, but it is a disaster if
your brain has ceased to keep pace
with your boots..."

This quote was attributed to Dr. Edwin P. Maynard in the American Medical Association publication, *A Physician's Guide to Gearing Up for Retirement* (1983, AMA). The major reason for selling is retirement. However, most doctors postpone this decision for as long as possible. The closer you get to retirement, the more likely you are to postpone the date. Younger doctors invariably plan on retiring earlier than older ones. However, as they grow older, this date will probably be pushed into the future.

If you are planning on selling your practice, whether for retirement or other personal reasons, it is critical to ask yourself several key questions and to answer them as honestly as possible.

- Why are you selling?
- What are you going to do if you sell?

- Are you ready to sell?
- If not, what is holding you back?
- Are you ready to set a target date?
- Will you be able to develop a new identity in retirement?

WHY AM I AFRAID OF SELLING MY PRACTICE?

There are many emotional barriers to overcome before you will be ready to sell your practice. For most clients, the overriding concern is that their patients continue to receive the best care possible. This concern is paramount for a successful changeover. It can also be a problem. Many practitioners cannot give up their practices, and thus interfere with the changeover. This interference is to the detriment of the entire transaction. Selling your practice, after years of nurturing it, can be like giving up a child to adulthood, or like the death of a spouse. Recognizing this is the first step to gaining emotional satisfaction with your decision.

HOW DO I START THE CHANGE PROCESS?

Change is difficult to start because of FEAR. FEAR is defined as False Evidence Appearing Real. FEAR results in anxiety, which is the psychological pain caused by fear. The first step in the change process is to reduce this level of anxiety.

How can FEAR create anxiety? The following may shed some light on this topic.

- All fears are learned; for example, a baby's only fear is height.

- The lack of knowledge creates anxiety.
- Lack of planning creates ambiguity, which results in anxiety.
- There may be a value conflict.
- There may be a problem with self image.

FEAR also creates an avoidance behavior. For example, you are told that at the end of a long hall there are two doors. Behind one door is a man-eating tiger. The other door opens to a pot of $1,000,000 in tax-free money. Most of us would walk down the hall with the expectation of receiving $1,000,000. However, part way down we hear a loud growl coming from behind the doors. All of a sudden our courage is dissipated, we back up, and vacillate between going ahead and leaving. This is an avoidance behavior caused by FEAR.

How is this overcome? The first step is recognizing the value of knowledge. Earlier I mentioned that many clients are thinking about retiring in the future, but after they have an appraisal done, all of a sudden they want to retire yesterday. This is an example of the value facts have in overcoming anxiety. Therefore, to start the change process it is important to get as much knowledge about the practice sale process as possible. Reading this book is an important step. Getting an appraisal done is the next step. Talking to a colleague, consultant or practice broker would be the next logical step. By then, you should be less anxious about the process because of the knowledge that you have gained.

It is helpful to have your spouse, if you have one, involved in the practice sale. Generally your spouse is concerned about what you will do in the future. This concern may show itself as anxiety about the various aspects of the practice sale, but the real concern is for the future of the couple. Knowledge about the practice disposition process helps relieve some of this anxiety. Many times I go to the home of a client after completing an appraisal and review the sale process with the spouse. These are very rewarding sessions. In one instance the spouse was crying because of the emotional stress that had been taken from her based upon knowledge about the practice sale process. With this out of the way, the spouse was able to confront the future and make plans to cope with it.

HOW DO I PLAN FOR RETIREMENT?

One of the best pieces of advice that I have heard is to consider retirement as a second career. Plan for it as you would any career change.

It is helpful to ease into the transition. If you are in the office four days a week now, perhaps through more efficient scheduling you could maintain the practice with three or three and one-half days in the office. This increases your out-of-office time and enables you to get a feel for retirement. If you have not had a long absence from the practice, perhaps a colleague or a locum tenens could be found to maintain the practice for a few weeks. Again, this is another way of "testing" retirement.

The second career aspect of retirement is fascinating. Perhaps you have a hobby or avocation that could be enhanced with more time. One client is going back to college and taking Western American history. He has an excellent collection of Old West memorabilia and is planning on writing a book about this subject. Another client is entering real estate development. He is taking courses now for his license and is starting his first project. Still another client is trying to launch his new career as a cruise ship doctor. All of these retiring doctors have entered retirement as a second career, not as a slowing down of the living process.

Retirement is a learning situation. It has taken a lifetime to learn your work behavior; now spend some time learning to be retired. The resultant drop in anxiety will be very pleasing.

Another source of anxiety, value conflict and self image resolution, can also be addressed. The first six months after the practice sale are the most difficult for the seller. If retirement is involved, a natural grieving process seems to occur. After six to twelve months of adjustment, the seller is launched into a new career or personal pathway. Once this occurs, the thought of going back to the practice is more of a problem than staying away from it. When this happens, the selling process is complete.

The problem of not being able to give up the practice is another good reason to use the resources of advisers. When there are after-sale questions from the buyer, or seller, the *sale contract* becomes the focus of attention. It can avert many problems, since a good attorney and practice consultant will insure that it contains documenta-tion to handle almost all after-sale problems.

Many successful practice changeovers occur when the seller remains with the practice, but on a reduced time basis. This is generally for a day or two per week, with a gradually reducing schedule. It is important that the seller comes back into the practice as an associate or employee, not as an owner. The buyer will be making changes in the practice, and the seller naturally will want to have an impact on them, but this is not good for the future of the practice. It is a good idea for the association to be on a voluntary basis, because the seller sometimes can sabotage the buyer emotionally. When this occurs, it is critical that the buyer get the seller out of the practice. Having the seller stay with the practice can enhance the changeover with patients, but it is important that the seller not maintain a say in the future management of the practice.

The AMA guide referenced at the beginning of this chapter suggests that you perform the following assessment about your physical and mental abilities before considering retirement:

- Physical Evaluation
     Strength, endurance, mobility
     Dexterity, coordination
     Vision, hearing
- Mental Evaluation
     Judgment
     Initiative
     Ability to get along with others
     Ability to keep up, learn and retain new
          knowledge

This publication also suggests that retirement can offer a number of advantages that can outweigh the desirability of continuing practice:

- Leaving while still respected for knowledge and abilities
- Time to maintain and cultivate family relationships and friendships
- More free time for avocations
- Greater freedom in your schedule
- Time to devote to a new career
- Fewer practice management worries

WHAT ABOUT A CAREER CHANGE?

Many doctors sell their practices because they want to change careers and do not want to retire. These mid-life career changes are very difficult for doctors because of the inordinate amount of time and money that have been devoted to education and training. However, the above advice also applies to a career change. I have had two clients who sold their practices in their forties and fifties, started a second career, then came back a few months later and purchased a practice. Others enjoy their new careers. The key to success is in maintaining a certain degree of flexibility for future events.

As a summary, it is important to remember that every person and every practice is unique. Whatever your circumstances, overcoming FEAR with knowledge and creative planning will pay off both financially and emotionally.

Now that the seller is ready for the practice sale, let's examine some of the FEARs that affect the buyer's purchase decision. These False Evidences Appearing Real also create anxiety on the buyer's side.

WHY AM I AFRAID OF BUYING A PRACTICE?

There are two basic reasons why many buyers are afraid to take the plunge and purchase a practice or buy into a group or partnership. The first reason is the fear of practice failure. The new doctor does not have a solid experience level, both clinically and emotionally, to see beyond the initial purchase decision. Purchasing a practice is by far the most economically feasible way of starting into practice. Only a very small percentage of these practice purchases actually result in business failures. I personally have never had a practice failure, but it certainly can happen. However, the facts indicate that the fear of practice failure is based upon false assumptions, not actual facts.

The second reason is the fear of another debt commitment. A graduating physician will have an average medical school debt of close to $30,000. The thought of going into debt for another $100,000 to purchase a practice appears to be insanity. Usually, a family is in the making, adding even more to the debt anxiety.

HOW CAN I PREVENT A PRACTICE FAILURE?

First, the facts indicate that a very small percentage of practice purchases actually fail. If you are buying into a group with an established track record, the percentage of failure is almost zero. What is more likely to occur in a group or partnership practice is the split-up of the doctors, which can mean the failure of the entire group. Generally, some of the doctors will reform into a smaller group, and others will join new practices or practice solo. A doctor rarely actually fails financially.

Chapter Nine, The Successful Transition, will go into detail concerning the right way to transfer patient goodwill to the buyer. Following the principles in that chapter almost certainly will guarantee success.

WHAT ABOUT LOCATION?

From an emotional standpoint, a bad situation can result from buying a practice in a location that is not compatible with your lifestyle. This also can occur when an important person who may be a part of your future life is not consulted or does not like the new location. The location also should reflect your practice philosophy.

First of all, the location decision reflects your practice philosophy, availability and accessibility. Answer the following questions to improve the likelihood of choosing a compatible location:

- What is the current competition for patients?
- What are the demographic characteristics of the area?

    Number of households

    Urban versus rural

    Area size and growth pattern

    Population age

    Average family size

    Average family income

- Age, number of years in practice, and location of competition?
- Availability of trained staff and suppliers?
- Living conditions?
- Availability of continuing education?
- Referral patterns and availability of subspecialists?
- Hospital availability and reputation?

From a personal standpoint, consider answers to the following:

- What part of the country would you like to live in?
- What is the quality of life?

- What is the potential for your spouse to work or pursue career or educational interests?
- Will the location meet your income objectives, both now and in the future?

Choosing a compatible location will give you a psychological advantage when it comes to working through any problems that may occur with the practice. A poor location decision will undermine the willpower that may be needed to work through potential problems. It then becomes easier to move away from the problems, instead of tackling them head on.

I DO NOT WANT TO GO FURTHER INTO DEBT.

The fear of excessive debt is the second major fear to overcome. Adding a practice purchase debt of $100,000 + to any existing education loans, car loans or home mortgages may result in a debt load that seems insurmountable. The problem with this fear is that people do not differentiate between personal debt and business debt. A business debt is undertaken in order to purchase or build a business. For a professional, a practice purchase debt is created in order to practice medicine and reap the financial rewards from private practice, either solo or group.

With a properly structured solo practice buy-out or group buy-in, the income from the practice will generate enough cash to provide personal living expenses and to retire the practice debt. This is a wise business decision. It makes more sense than borrowing $100,000 and starting a scratch practice that does not guarantee an income large enough to provide both of these results. For example, with the usual practice purchase, enough funds are generated from the practice, in excess of reasonable personal living expenses, to pay off the practice debt, plus interest, within five years.

The key is reasonable personal living expenses. If you decide to radically change your lifestyle after school with the purchase of a new home, luxury car, exotic vacations, and country club membership, then the practice probably will not generate enough funds to support this new lifestyle plus pay off the practice debt. The key is being conservative until the financial results indicate a more liberal personal lifestyle. By postponing this lifestyle gratification for a few years, you will have an even better lifestyle in the future.

Many insurance companies and financial consultants use the following financial planning pyramid shown in Figure 6 to demonstrate a logical sequence for personal financial planning. This pyramid of investment planning is an excellent tool for anyone. By starting at the bottom and taking care of immediate practice and personal needs, protection is provided at the least cost. As disposable income increases, the financial planning process moves up the pyramid to speculative investments. Many doctors are notorious for making poor investments, and the mistake that most of them make is that they jump to the apex of the pyramid—the speculation phase—before taking care of basic needs.

You will notice that practice debt does not appear in the pyramid. To find its position, the foundation (INCOME), needs to be expanded (Figure 7). This can be done with a cash flow diagram for the typical practice.

Operating income is the cash left over in the practice after practice expenses have been paid. Expenses do not include depreciation, since this is not a cash flow expense, interest on practice debts, retirement plan funding, or doctor's salary. The operating income can then be expanded as shown in Figure 8.

Figure 6
FINANCIAL PLANNING PYRAMIND

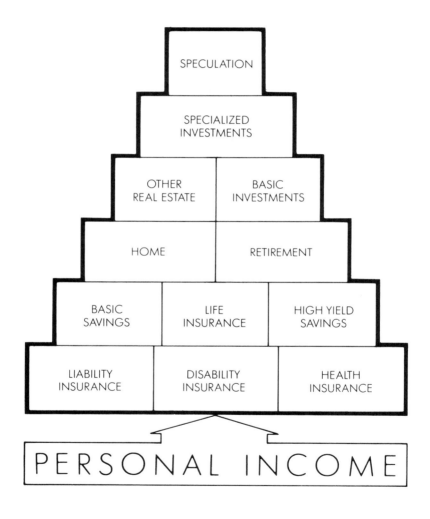

Figure 7

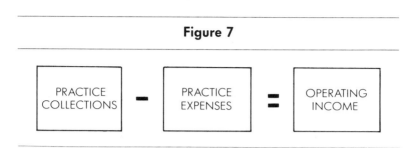

A buyer's take home pay is determined by what is left over after payments for the practice and income taxes have been deducted from cash operating income. With good planning, most of the practice buy-out debt can be deductible, so that income taxes are minimized. Thus, a well-structured and planned practice purchase must be able to support the buyer's personal income needs plus make the buy-out payments. If the potential practice or group buy-in does not meet these two criteria, the decision to purchase should not be made.

Financial planning during the transition phase of the buy-out also is important. In many cases, the buyer must wait for his or her own receivables to be collected before seeing any cash in the practice. The buyer usually gets a bank loan for working capital before purchasing the practice. Working capital (generally two to three months of business plus personal expenses) lets the new owner pay

Figure 8

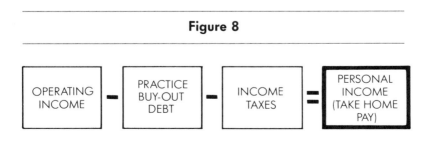

expenses before collections from insurance companies and patients are received. Many sellers will assist buyers during this critical financial juncture. Common steps are to postpone practice buy-out payments for up to six months, to reduce rent payments (if renting a buyer-owned facility) for the first few months, or to include accounts receivable in the practice sale. More information on this will be given in Chapter Eight, Legal and Financial Considerations.

In summary, from a buyer's perspective a practice purchase is an excellent financial planning decision. The practice most likely will not fail and the buyer will be able to pay off the practice purchase debt without committing financial hari kari. The result will be a doctor getting a head start in his or her clinical and financial career. Depending upon the size of the practice purchased, the buyer will be in excellent financial shape only a few years after the purchase. At this stage, moving up the financial planning pyramid will be fun.

Remember, FEAR (False Evidence Appearing Real) can be eliminated with a few simple facts. Reducing the anxiety caused by FEAR will make the emotional process simpler and more rewarding for both sellers and buyers.

3

PRACTICE VALUATION

"The word value is not a crystal, transparent and unchanged; it is the skin of a living thought, and may vary greatly in color and content according to the circumstances and the time in which it is used."

Oliver Wendell Holmes, Associate Justice of the Supreme Court, used the above quote to describe the concept of value (Towne v. Eisner, 245 U.S. 418). The purpose of this chapter is to explain how a value is established for a practice. Even though a practice may have a market value, this does not guarantee that the practice will eventually sell, or that it will sell at the market value. The *final sale price* is determined by many factors, which will be understood as this chapter is completed.

A market value is placed on a professional practice after an appraisal has been done. However, value is a word with many meanings. It is the symbol of ideas and cannot be defined precisely. Value pertains to the relationship between something that is desired and a potential purchaser. Four factors influence value:

Desire: Desire for an object contributes to its value. This desire is not sufficient by itself to create value. For example, food is valuable to satisfy hunger. However, if you have twice the amount of food that you need to satisfy your hunger, the excess food has little value.

Utility: The ability to satisfy a need or desire determines the usefulness of the item. Bread has greater utility to a hungry person than to someone who is not hungry.

Scarcity: Scarcity must accompany desire and utility before a value can exist. For example, air has great utility, but it is not scarce. However, if you are a scuba diver, then air can become a very scarce commodity.

Purchasing Power: Purchasing power enables a person to satisfy desire. Thus, purchasing power enables someone to satisfy a desire for an object that has scarcity and utility. This produces value.

Utility, scarcity, desire, and purchasing power together are prerequisites to value. Thus, an appraisal does not make value; it interprets it based on market evidence. Professional practices have value. They meet the requirements of utility, scarcity and purchasing power.

WHY SHOULD I HAVE A PROFESSIONAL APPRAISAL DONE?

The purpose of an appraisal is to provide an estimate of value. When an appraisal is based on personal opinions unsupported by market research or knowledge, the quality of the appraisal is very questionable. The definition of an appraisal is: "An opinion of value for adequately described property, as of a specified date, supported by the analysis of relevant data." The reliability of an appraisal depends on the basic competence and integrity of the appraiser, the availability of data, and the skill with which the data is assembled and processed.

Many people can give *opinions* as to the value of a practice. However, to have meaning, the opinion should go beyond any personal feeling of the appraiser. It should be based solely on competence and facts.

The appraisal requires selective research into the appropriate market area; the assembly of pertinent data; application of appropriate analytic techniques; and knowledge, experience and professional judgment necessary to develop a conclusion that is appropriate to the problem.

The critical factor is professional judgment. Appraising is not an exact science. A good appraiser will form a conclusion that recognizes the difference between personal opinions, observed facts and professional judgment.

The appraisal should list the assets and the goodwill value of the practice. In addition, a well-done appraisal will point out positive and negative attributes of the practice and how they impact on the final valuation. For this reason, it's a good idea to have an appraisal done a few months or years before the practice is offered for sale. In this way you will have time to make changes that increase the value and salability of the practice.

Keep in mind that there is a distinction between market value and final sale price. The price (market value) asked for a practice and the price at which the practice finally sells may not bear any relationship to each other. A final price may reflect caprice, unequal motivation or negotiating position, unusual terms, or other factors that cause the final sale price to deviate from market value. Thus, just because you know what the practice down the street sold for, it may bear no resemblance to what *your* practice is actually worth.

WHAT IS THE BUYER-SELLER SUBJECTIVE VALUE CONCEPT?

A Buyer-Seller Subjective Value Concept curve (Figure 9) best explains the relationship that takes place to determine a market value for a practice. The top curve represents the seller's subjective value line. The horizontal axis is time, the vertical axis money. At first, the seller decides that the practice should have a value of one year's gross revenue plus replacement value for equipment (Point A). No sale will take place. Why? Because the *buyer's* subjective value line (bottom curve) does not intersect with the seller's curve. In this instance, the buyer decides that the practice has no value for goodwill or equipment—a price of zero. No sale takes place.

Figure 9

**BUYER-SELLER
SUBJECTIVE VALUE CONCEPT**

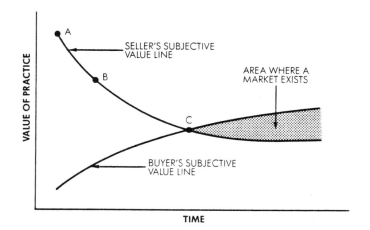

With no takers for the practice the seller decides to lower his value to perhaps nine months of goodwill plus market value for equipment (Point B). Again, no sale takes place. Finally, the seller decides to place a reasonable value on the practice. Also, at this time, a buyer appears on the scene who agrees with this value for the practice. This represents the intersection of the two curves (Point C). Any value lower than this will bring in more interested buyers, which is the shaded area of the graph. This shaded area represents the area in which a market for the practice exists.

As a seller, your goal should be to value your practice at the junction of the two curves. This represents the most economically beneficial value for both buyer and seller. It should also represent the final sale price if other aspects of the practice are present to conclude the transaction.

Since this curve has a horizontal axis representing time, sellers can lose a lot of time if their practices are not valued correctly. During this time when no sale will occur, the average doctor may let his or her practice dwindle, and the final value may be even more depressed. Buyers also need to be aware that if they are looking for a "bargain basement" price for a practice, they may waste a lot of valuable time searching for a practice that does not exist.

WHAT ARE THE WAYS TO VALUE A PRACTICE?

There are many approaches to valuing a practice. Some of the more common ones are as follows:

- Rule of thumb
- Cost

- Income
- Market data

No one technique should be relied upon solely. It is best to use a variety of approaches and cross-check the results. Invariably, the best method to use will become evident after all aspects of the practice valuation situation have been determined and analyzed.

Because of the complexities involved, along with the chance that incorrect assumptions can result in costly mistakes, it is not possible to demonstrate accurately how to value *your* practice or clinic in this book. What will be shown is information about the various methods used by professional practice appraisers. With this information you can gain an idea of the approximate valuation of your specific practice situation and judge appraisal reports done by others. Accordingly, buyers should use the information in a like manner.

The *rule of thumb* method should never be used to value a practice accurately. By definition, a rule of thumb is used only to estimate a number, not to define the number accurately. For example, CPAs invariably use the rule of thumb of one year's gross collections to value a medical or dental practice. My own court testimony in marriage dissolution trials easily refutes this indicator of practice worth, much to the satisfaction of the doctor's attorney. Rules of thumb do not take into account the individual differences in practices and clinics. They underestimate the value of well-managed practices and overvalue the worth of poorly-managed ones. As stated before in this book, every practice is unique; therefore, why not recognize this uniqueness? Rules of thumb have no place in an accurate and professional valuation of a practice or clinic.

The *cost method* is used by many doctors when they leave a group or add new members. Equipment, instruments, supplies, and accounts receivable values are estimated; liabilities deducted; and then this value is multiplied by the percentage ownership of each of the partners or shareholders. No value is given to goodwill. This is excellent for the new person joining a group, but not for the seller. The most significant portion of most valuations is goodwill, which is not included in the cost method of determining value. However, this is the main reason that a practice has value—the goodwill developed over the years and reflected in active patient flow. More and more medical groups are becoming aware of this, and older partnership and corporate buy-out agreements are beginning to be revised to reflect the new realities.

Another approach to valuation, the *income method*, sometimes is used to value professional practices. However, it may not apply to most solo practices and small groups. The income approach method may be applicable to an urgent care clinic, hospital, nursing home, or a large clinic. The principle behind this method is that the entity has "excess income" which is multiplied by a capitalization factor to determine value. For example, an urgent care clinic may have $50,000 per year after taxes, when all expenses and salaries have been paid. Assuming that the owner, or owners, do not contribute significant personal production to the gross income, then a new owner could purchase the urgent care clinic, be an absentee owner, and still receive a yearly income from the clinic. This yearly income might be valued from four to six times earnings, depending on the current interest rates and future likelihood of profits. Thus a value of $200,000 (four times $50,000) to $300,000 (six times $50,000) might be placed on this clinic. This value would include all assets, lia-

bilities and accounts receivable. However, for most practices, excess income is not generated. The owner (doctor)
does personal production, pays expenses, and receives
what is left over as income. Since most practices have
similar production, expense, and net income percentages,
there usually is no excess income.

For example, in a recent divorce case, the appraiser for
the physician's spouse was not familiar with medical
clinics. He used the excess income approach to value the
physician's share of the three-person family practice clinic.
The excess income was calculated to be $20,000, based on
the fact that the physician earned about $20,000 more per
year than his two colleagues. An artificially high value was
placed on his practice because of this. However, my
examination indicated that the physician, even though he
earned more than his partners, was still below the national
average for net income for his specialty. A more thorough
analysis, based on a critical examination of the facts,
resulted in a lower value for the practice. In this case, this
was helpful to the physician, since the final divorce
settlement was more in line with the actual value of the
practice.

Roger Hill and James Jackson, DDS, in their book *New
Trends in Dental Practice Valuation and Associateship
Arrangements* (Quintessence Publishing Co., 1987), use a
capitalization rate to convert a stream of earnings into a
practice value. This earnings approach is being used in the
valuation of professional practices for several reasons.
First, as more doctors are being employed as employees,
rather than partners, an accurate estimate of doctors'
compensation rates can be made. Second, it takes some of
the "art" out of practice valuations and makes it more of a
replicable "science."

To explain this capitalization of income method, the
example shown in Figure 10 was taken from their book. It

will be used to explain the various concepts and assumptions used with this technique.

Figure 10

CAPITALIZATION OF INCOME METHOD

Projected Professional Income	$221,623
Cost of Professional Services	(63,000)
Operating Expenses	(121,893)
Interest Income	0
Interest Expense	(30)
Depreciation	(517)
Profit After Tax	36,183
Estimated Tax	(5,513)
Profit After Tax	$30,670
Capitalization Rate	18%
Fair Market Value $30,670.18 =	$170,390

This example started with the gross collections of the practice, and subtracted the following items:

- The cost of compensating a doctor to produce the expected income ($63,000)
- The operating expenses ($121,893)
- Interest income
- Interest expense ($30)
- Depreciation charges ($517)
- Estimated taxes (estimates are based on corporate tax rates, irrespective of whether the practice is actually incorporated)

The resulting after-tax income of $30,670 represents an amount of incremental earnings available only to the owner/operator of the practice. The income producer in this example was paid $63,000. If the income producer and the owner/operator are the same, he would receive $93,670 ($63,000 + $30,670 = $93,670).

The value arrived at for the practice includes all assets of the practice (furniture, equipment, instruments, supplies and accounts receivable).

The capitalization rate, 18%, must be properly selected. The capitalization rate has at least three components. They are as follows:

Risk-free rate of return: This is the risk-free rate of return that a person could be assured of receiving in an investment opportunity. The best benchmark would be treasury notes or long-term government bonds.

Liquidity: This is the consideration of the liquidity or the illiquidity of the investment in a professional practice. Very little reliable information exists to indicate the amount that should be included in this component. Typically, this may represent 3 to 5 percentage points.

Risk: The third component is the factor for the risk involved in the purchase decision. This can be subdivided into individual practice risk and general overall economic conditions risk. This may represent 4 to 12 percentage points.

Generally, the capitalization rate can vary from about 15% to 25%. For this example, 18% was used. Honing in on an accurate estimate of the capitalization rate is difficult, and should be left in the hands of a professional appraiser.

The most frequently used valuation method is the *market data* approach. Basically, this value is based on

what similar practices in the area have sold for in the past.
Using the market data approach summarizes the results of
many separate decisions made by buyers, sellers, and
other doctors who may have thought of starting a practice.

The market data approach is essentially the same
system used by residential home appraisers. The value of a
home is dependent upon what similar homes in the
neighborhood have sold for in the past. The overall real
estate market has an impact—plus interest rates, housing
availability, and future economic projections for the area.
However, all these conditions are reflected in the value.
Since a home does not produce excess income, the income
approach is not used. However, if there is a duplex that is
rented, or a commercial property, then the income method is probably the best way to determine value.

I have used the income approach to value large physical
therapy clinics and large medical clinics. In other instances I have used it to check the market value approach.
As a seller or buyer, you need to understand when each
method of valuation can be used and what applies to your
specific situation.

One mistake to avoid is to use each approach and then
average them. This is like asking three people for the
correct time and averaging their replies. You want to
decide which technique is the most reliable, and put more
weight on it. In most cases, market value is best, perhaps
with some influence by the income method.

Market value can have its pitfalls. For example, one
doctor had an excessive amount of equipment in his office.
By adding up goodwill, equipment and accounts receivable, an unusually high value was obtained. However, the
value was not justified based upon the net income from
the practice. A buyer would not be able to utilize all the
equipment assets of the practice in an efficient manner. In

order to sell this practice, it was necessary to discount the price of the equipment assets.

The market value approach separately values tangible items (physical assets and accounts receivable) from the intangible goodwill, and then adds them all together.

HOW DO I VALUE PHYSICAL ASSETS?

Physical assets are considered equipment, instruments, furniture, and office and clinical supplies. The assets should be inventoried and a competent appraiser contacted to estimate market value. If your practice contains only fairly new equipment (less than three years old), then the depreciated book value may be realistic. However, in most practices book value does not equal market value. Book value generally is much lower than the market value of the assets.

In addition to a qualified appraiser, equipment sales and marketing personnel usually can give reliable estimates of equipment market values. It should be remembered that "book value," "depreciated value" and other accounting techniques used for tax purposes usually are not accurate reflections of the actual market value of equipment and furniture. The final value is determined by what other physicians or dentists are willing to pay for the used assets.

Supplies and minor instruments can be inventoried, although using two to three months' worth of supply expenses is a good estimate. Be careful not to spend too much time "counting the sponges" and getting involved in inventory hassles with a new buyer. Supplies are a *minor part* of most practices, and thus deserve little priority. I have seen a case where an argument over the value of a box of syringes negated a potential $100,000 practice sale. Try to maintain your perspective.

WHAT IS THIS THING CALLED GOODWILL?

Goodwill is defined as "the expectation of future profits under the ownership of someone other than the present owner." This is a widely accepted definition by both accounting standards and the Internal Revenue Service ruling, 59-60.

Goodwill usually is the most valuable part of a practice. However, it is not stated on the balance sheet because you are the major asset. You bring all the physical and personal assets of your practice together in a way to enhance its value. Goodwill is the payback for all those years of nurturing patients, consoling staff, fighting with bankers and filling out government forms. It is summarized by the trust that your patients have in your clinical and personal decisions.

The goodwill of a practice is almost impossible to evaluate by yourself. An outside expert probably can assign a much higher value for your practice based on a professional evaluation of goodwill. On the other side of the coin, many doctors have inflated and unrealistic ideas about the value of their goodwill. In these instances, self-determined goodwill will probably result in no practice sale, as buyers will not pay inflated prices for practices.

WHAT FACTORS MAKE UP GOODWILL?

Many factors go into determining the goodwill of the practice. If you know what factors determine goodwill, and if you plan far enough ahead, then this part of the practice valuation can be maximized. The following areas should be considered:

Location

- The location of the practice is very important. Ideally it should be in a modern office complex with ease of access for patients. Many older doctors are the last ones to leave a changing neighborhood or a deteriorating office building. This detracts from the value of the practices. Although moving may seem to be a difficult task, it might pay off with a more comfortable retirement later.

- For example, in a recent estate sale, the only way to dispose of a practice was to have another doctor purchase the patient charts and move them to his location. The deceased doctor's office was closed down and the equipment disposed of. The building was so old that the plumbing necessary for new equipment was not available. Patients had to walk up a long flight of stairs, since there was no elevator available.

- A recently graduated doctor purchased a practice in a deteriorating neighborhood. He only had to pay for the equipment, because of the poor location. One year later, as he drove up to my office in a new sports car, he stated that he wanted to sell his practice. It was located in a "combat zone," and even though he was making significantly more than his school colleagues, the stress of practicing in the location was too much. The practice will be very difficult to sell because of the location.

- One thing to remember, as a buyer, is that location is not the most critical aspect to evaluate when purchasing a practice. Most doctors want to locate in neighborhoods that have a good quality of life, cultural activities, sports events, recreational facilities, and a rapidly growing population. For example, Phoenix is one of the fastest-growing cities in the United States. However, if this growth is based on elderly patients, an obstetrician may not see too much growth. Even in locations where the economy is devastated I have found practices that are very successful and growing. The most important variable is not location, but the skill of the doctor in developing a thriving practice.

Type of Practice

- In general, a subspecialty practice which has a high percentage of patient referrals from other doctors is valued less than a primary care or general practice. This is because a subspecialist may see a patient only once, and not for routine ongoing care. This lowers the value of the patient flow. If you have a referral practice, try to maintain your referral network and add new and younger doctors to it.

- For example, one subspecialist in a small city only had two referring doctors left in his practice. Before I could complete the appraisal one of these doctors announced his retirement. The value of the goodwill probably was cut in half by this retirement.

Patient Demographics

- Try to maintain a good mix of all age groups in the practice. Younger patients, families, and patients with higher incomes usually are more valuable than practices with older patients.

Staff

- The staff is an integral part of goodwill. Positive factors include well-trained staff members, personable employees, and their length of time with the practice. The receptionist may be the most important person in the office. Most patients and referral sources know the receptionist better than they know the doctor. Continuity of the staff with the new buyer is critical, since the staff adds a familiar link for the patient with the practice after the seller leaves.

- The practice of a deceased doctor was held together solely by the receptionist until a new doctor could be found to assume the practice. In another example, a disabled doctor was able to maintain patients until the practice sold because of the actions of the receptionist.

Financial

- The better the financial shape of the practice, the more it will be worth. Important "vital signs" to consider are gross annual production, collection ratio, and net income as a percentage of collections. Remember, a buyer needs to live off the net income from the practice plus make payments to you or a bank for the practice purchase price. The higher the practice net income, the more the value for the goodwill.

Non-Compete Clause

- Most buyers will insist on this so that the seller cannot set up another practice down the street and siphon off patients. The seller's willingness to sign such a clause increases the value of the practice. The clause needs to be reasonable, however. Usually this does not preclude the seller from working for an HMO or government agency where patients are preselected.

Transition

■ It is very helpful for the buyer if the seller will remain for a certain time after the sale. The purpose of this is to introduce patients and referring doctors to the buyer. The transition period plays an important role in the successful transfer of the goodwill of the practice to the buyer.

HOW MUCH IS GOODWILL WORTH?

This is the most frequently asked question in my seminars. The answer is another question. "What will it cost to have my toothache fixed?" If you are a dentist, you cannot answer that except by saying that it might take two aspirin, or it might require a three-unit porcelain/gold crown bridge, or even years of periodontal treatment. A dentist only can give a definite answer after an exam is completed and, probably, x-rays taken. The same is true for goodwill. Every practice is unique, and since goodwill is a complex, multi-faceted area, a thorough analysis of the individual practice needs to be done. Setting your own value on goodwill based on what the practice down the street sold for could result in thousands of dollars of lost potential value.

The actual value of goodwill varies from zero to a few months of practice collections. In some instances a goodwill value of one year's gross revenue may be recommended, but I have never seen a practice that financially could justify this high a goodwill factor. Accountants sometimes use one year's gross, because that seems to be a common valuation for accounting practices. However, at present, this does not apply to health care practices.

An article in *Medical Economics* (October 19, 1984) put an average value on medical practice goodwill of 22% of annual collections. This varied widely by specialty. In my experience, an average of three to six months of gross collections is more accurate. The value of goodwill has risen over the past few years.

It is critical to remember that all the factors previously mentioned—location, type of practice, patient demographics, staff, financial health, non-compete clause, and assistance during the changeover—have an impact on the final goodwill valuation for the individual practice. One thing is certain: there is no such thing as an *average* practice. Each practice is unique and must be evaluated from that standpoint.

Courts sometimes use different assumptions in valuing goodwill. For example, I am called upon many times to act as an expert witness in marriage dissolution trials. In some states professional practices have goodwill; in others they do not. For example, the Nebraska Supreme Court ruled on May 16, 1986 (Taylor v. Taylor, 386 N.W.2d 581), that there was no goodwill in a physician's business. This was because the business (laboratory plus practice) depended upon the continued presence of the physician. To be property that could be divided and distributed in a dissolution proceeding, goodwill must be a business asset with a value independent of the presence or reputation of a particular person; an asset that may be sold, transferred, conveyed, or pledged, the Supreme Court said.

On the other hand, in 1985 the New York Supreme Court awarded a physician's ex-wife a share of his future earnings. She earned this share of the value of his license, the court said, when she put him through medical school. Each individual state will consider goodwill differently for dissolutions. However, actual practice sales indicate that there is a value for the "blue sky" portion of a practice, independent of court results.

Since there is simply no well-defined market for buying and selling practices, there is no sure pricing formula. Each sale transaction is isolated from others according to the practice's unique characteristics and the results of individual negotiating sessions. The appraisal of the value of goodwill is, unfortunately, still an art; not a science.

WHAT ABOUT VALUING PATIENT CHARTS?

Some appraisers place a value on individual patient charts as the basis for a goodwill valuation. The problems with this technique are the following:

- It is very difficult to define "active patients." For example, are active patients those who are on a recall system; have been in for an appointment in the past year, two years, three years or more; or may not have been in for years but could call any day for an appointment? What about a subspecialty practice that does not provide chronic care?

- It does not take into account the various aspects of goodwill already discussed.

Using only patient charts as the method of goodwill valuation may be inaccurate and is subject to various interpretations. For these reasons, I prefer the number of months of collections as the basis for goodwill valuation. After the practice sale price has been determined between buyer and seller, then it may be appropriate to assign a value to patient charts if this is needed for financial reasons.

The best way to point out the danger of using a rule of thumb ratio to evaluate goodwill across the board is with the following example:

> Two practices are grossing $180,000 each. The doctors independently read that four months was an average goodwill figure. So they independently chose a goodwill value of $60,000 ($15,000/month times 4) for their respective practices. One practice sold very quickly; the other stayed on the market until outside professional help was obtained to move the practice.

Why did one practice sell quickly and the other did not? The key factor was *net income*. The first practice, which sold quickly, had a very low overhead. The doctor was making about $20,000 per year more than his colleagues. The buyer for this practice quickly recognized that he was getting it for a steal, and bought it before the selling doctor realized that he was priced too low. The second doctor had a high overhead. He was making about $20,000 per year *less* than his colleagues. Potential buyers realized that he had priced his practice too high to sell, so the practice dwindled while the doctor frantically searched for potential buyers.

The spread between actual goodwill values could have been up to $60,000 for these two "identical" practices. This example is only for one aspect of goodwill—the financial health of the practice. Each of the goodwill areas needs to be examined and the results integrated into the final goodwill valuation. Thus, no practice is average; every practice is unique. In the end, it is your money and time that may be wasted because of an inaccurate goodwill appraisal. As you can see, using gross income as the single major factor in appraising goodwill with a simple formula is misleading, and could be expensive.

WHAT ABOUT MY ACCOUNTS RECEIVABLE?

Accounts receivable are another major asset in a practice. They normally are not included in an appraisal since they represent income that has not been collected by the seller. Usually, the seller keeps the accounts receivable, and has the buyer collect them. A small collection fee usually is paid to reimburse the buyer for staff time required to collect receivables. On some occasions, the receivables may be purchased as part of the practice. When this occurs, valuing the receivables becomes important.

To value accounts receivable, it is necessary to age them. Aging merely means separating the receivables from the amount of time the production was done. For example, a $90.00 billing that has not been paid for two months would be a sixty-day account. By aging the receivables, you will be able to better determine which ones may get paid and which ones may result in a bad debt loss. Generally, the longer the time the receivable has been on the books, the less likelihood of collecting the entire amount.

In a well-managed practice, receivables should be less than three to three and one-half times the average monthly production. For example, if average production is $20,000 per month, then receivables should not be more than $60,000 to $70,000. If they are more than this there may be a collections problem. Buyers look for well-managed offices, so a high accounts receivable number may scare some of them. On the other hand, if you never write off old accounts, but leave them on the books, then even though your receivables may be higher than average, the amount available for collection may be more in line with an average practice. Therefore, it is a good idea to clean up receivables before having an appraisal done. In this way, the practice will appear to be well-managed.

Receivables are valued after they have been aged. A percentage factor is applied to each aging period. For example, current receivables are more likely to be collected, so you may want to multiply current receivables by 90 to 95%. Receivables over three months old are not as likely to be collected. Here the factor may be 60 to 70%. As a rule, banks and financial institutions will multiply total receivables by about 65 to 75% to arrive at a loan collateral value. However, most health care practices are able to collect more than this. You and your staff are the most knowledgeable people concerning patient payment habits. You may want to review each account personally and place a probability on its being paid. The sum total would be the value of the accounts receivable.

An example of a complete practice appraisal is shown in Appendix A. By reading it, you can get a general idea of the market value approach to practice valuation.

WHERE CAN I GET AN APPRAISAL DONE?

Now that you understand the various aspects of your practice and how they impact on the final market value determination, you need to obtain that value. Many thousands of dollars and, indeed, even your financial well-being may depend on a proper valuation.

The first place many doctors start is with their accountant or CPA. This person can assist in obtaining the necessary information for the appraisal to proceed. Most appraisers will want to know gross income and expenses for the past two to three years (usually Schedule C tax returns of solo practices or a corporation or partnership return). Accounts receivable aging reports and an asset list with depreciation schedules usually will be required. Do not forget to add an estimated amount for instruments and supplies.

One word of caution: most accountants and CPAs are not involved actively with practice valuations. Rules of thumb used for valuing businesses, even CPA firms, usually do *not* apply to practices.

If you want to do the appraisal yourself, then the easiest part is the accounts receivable. After that, equipment, instruments, furniture, clinical supplies, and office supplies need to be valued. Clinical supply and equipment firms can assist in this.

The final area of valuation is goodwill. As you know, this usually is the largest part of the valuation and can represent over 50% of the total market value. It is not easily determined on your own. If you want to estimate it yourself, then talk to colleagues in your specialty who recently have sold their practices and find out what their goodwill values were. However, these values usually will have a very wide range, since each sale is unique. Also, it is extremely difficult to get reliable information. Have you ever asked your neighbors or colleagues what they paid for a new car? You will be shocked at the prices quoted to you, because everyone believes that they were able to get "the best deal" and even if they did not, do not want to admit that to you.

Once all the information is available, have it typed neatly so that the final document appears official and professional.

WHAT IF I USE A PROFESSIONAL APPRAISER?

If you decide to use a practice broker, management consultant, or appraiser, the key task is to select the right person. No matter whom you use, there should be no tie-in between the appraisal and follow-up business. You want an unbiased, professional evaluation of your practice to determine its market value. It is then a separate decision to have someone actively market the practice for you. It might be worthwhile to consider having two appraisals done, which is similar to getting a second opinion in a clinical case.

Key questions to ask the potential appraiser include the following:

- How long has the person been in business?
- Does the person specialize in valuing health care practices, or does he or she handle all types of businesses?
- If the person also sells practices, how close do the final sale prices come to the initial appraisal values?
- What is the person's education, training and experience?
- Does the appraisal commit you to any follow-up activity, such as listing the practice?
- What are the fees?
- What kind of references does the person have?
- Is the appraiser licensed or certified (if required in your state)?
- Has the appraiser had experience as an expert witness in court testimony?

■ How is confidentiality maintained?

The charge for appraisals can vary considerably, from free up to a few thousand dollars. The answers to the above questions will help to select the right person and determine the appropriateness of the fees.

Once the appraisal is completed, reread this section of the book and compare the comments in it with your appraisal. If the appraisal covers the basic areas of valuation and seems fair, then accept it. If not, and shortcuts or invalid assumptions appear to have been made, contact the appraiser to try to correct or to revise the document. If no satisfaction is obtained, it is time for a second opinion. Remember, the appraisal is your property; you can use it or not use it; the choice is yours.

Now that you have a realistic value determination for your practice, the next step is to decide how to sell the practice. If the appraisal is the end result, i.e., needed for estate planning, insurance, divorce settlement, etc., then you will not be taking the next step yet. In any case, a well done appraisal will indicate areas that need to be improved in your practice to enhance its value. If there is time, think about initiating some changes in the practice to improve its value. Then you may want to have another appraisal done, or an update of the existing appraisal. The result should be a higher value for the practice. Now would be the time to initiate the sale process.

Chapter Five will discuss ways to maximize practice valuation. Consider the ideas carefully. Any action taken should be considered an investment in your practice and ultimately in your retirement income.

Astute buyers should consider seriously having a practice appraised independently of the seller's appraisal. Second opinions are very valuable, and may provide more leverage in the sale price negotiations.

4

GROUPS, PARTNERSHIPS, CLINICS & CORPORATIONS

"What God hath joined together, let no man put asunder..."

Marriage vows and health care group agreements have a lot in common. Just like a marriage, they are easy to enter into, with grand hopes for the future. However, just like a divorce, they are more difficult to get out of without a lot of hurt feelings, trauma and expense.

About 80% of the physicians in private practice are in a group practice of some form or another. Dentists, on the contrary, do not like groups. Over 80% of private practice dentists are in solo practice. Thus the group phenomenon is almost exclusively physician-oriented.

If you are in solo practice, adding a partner is an excellent way of planning ahead for retirement. This makes sense if the senior doctor has too many patients and wants to cut down gradually on the patient load without letting the practice dwindle in value. It must be recognized that such a method of planning for retirement necessarily will result in lower income as the new partner absorbs some of these patients. Trouble occurs when the older doctor is not willing to risk existing income.

Many new physicians, when just out of school, may consider starting a partnership or group arrangement with other new colleagues. Whether this makes sense or not depends upon a lot of variables. For example, Martin L. Schulman, in his book *Medical Partnerships & Practice Disposition* (Praeger Publishers, 1983), suggests the following positive aspects:

Independence: The young doctors are free to establish the practice as they see fit, rather than accommodate their style or attitudes to some older doctors who expect new associates to adjust to their way of doing things.

Responsibility: The doctors are responsible for their own success or failure.

Dominance: The doctors are both "senior" doctors. This sense of being in charge, of being able to set the rules, and to run the practice exactly as they choose can be important to some physicians, even at this early stage in a professional career.

Easier Schedule: Partnership lessens the burdens of on-call commitments and vacation planning.

He goes on to point out significant risks to new doctor partnerships:

Financial Risk: Opening an office is an expensive business. All of this overhead must be supported without the benefit of an established patient base.

Lack of Relationship With Older Doctors: Despite the disadvantages of being a junior partner in an established practice, it can be a comfortable situation—emotionally and psychically. Someone is always around to ask, to watch, and to learn from.

Pressure to Succeed: Besides being a positive factor, the pressure to succeed can be tremendous, especially if it must be done immediately for financial survival.

Income Limiting: These young doctor partnerships generally result in less income in the early years than do junior partnerships in successful, established practices.

Thus, from a buy-in standpoint, the negative factors seem to outweigh the positive factors of starting partnerships and groups from scratch. As a potential buyer, it will probably be a better financial and emotional decision to buy in with an established solo doctor or an existing group with an older doctor getting ready to retire. Consider joining doctors or groups that seem to fit your style of practice—both clinically and emotionally.

The rest of this chapter will focus on the valuation and selling aspects of medical groups.

WHAT ARE SOME SPECIAL VALUATION CONSIDERATIONS?

Appraising medical groups consisting of the same subspecialty is very similar to the process we have just finished reading about. Generally, the group itself is considered as one practice. Once an appraisal value has been determined for physical assets, goodwill and accounts receivable, then these values can be allocated among the members using various formulas.

The most common group form is the practice expense-sharing arrangement. In this scenario the physicians have individual practices, but share some common overhead items, such as equipment ownership, business office personnel, reception area space, and possibly the facility ownership itself. The physical assets merely are divided up according to how the group members share ownership. For example, if two physicians each own their equipment and furniture equally, then the market value of the assets is divided equally between them. It also is common to find many groups where some equipment and furniture is jointly owned, such as an x-ray machine, with individual exam rooms and private offices furnished by each physician. Again, the market value for the assets is allocated per ownership rights.

Accounts receivable generally are kept separate for each member of the group. Thus, each physician's receivables can be valued separately.

Goodwill is a little more difficult to allocate. If there is an age discrepancy, the doctor who has been in practice longer can claim that more of the goodwill is due to his efforts than to a newer member of the group. In general, however, goodwill usually is allocated based upon each doctor's percentage of total collections. For example, Dr. A may collect $200,000 per year and Dr. B $300,000. Therefore, Dr. A would be allocated 40% of the goodwill ($200,000 divided by $500,000) and Dr. B. 60%.

Multispecialty groups and clinics are much more difficult to appraise and to determine individual physician ownership values. For example, a surgeon in an internal medicine or family practice group generally will produce more than the average physician in the group. The surgeon's expenses and equipment needs also generally will be less. However, the surgeon's goodwill is dependent upon the referrals from the others in the group, and thus is not easily transferable without the group's approval. In this instance, determining goodwill allocation is very difficult. It has to be analyzed on a group by group basis.

Professional corporations are treated the same as individual practices when appraising a group. Care has to be taken to keep assets separate for the various entities. For example, an individual physician may be incorporated, and his personal office furniture owned by the corporation. The medical equipment in the exam rooms may be owned jointly by the partnership or other arrangement governing the entire clinic. Keeping everything separate is very important when the individual practice is sold, so that corporate versus individual ownership and tax ramifications can be handled properly.

For a large clinic, usually with more than six physicians, the income method for valuing the entity usually is utilized. This is because the clinic is not dependent upon one or two physicians in order to be successful. In many instances, some of the physicians are employees or independent contractors, which complicates the appraisal if it is done with the market value approach. In such instances, the value usually is allocated based solely upon stock ownership percentages.

HOW ARE BUY-INS AND
BUY-OUTS
ACCOMPLISHED?

In my experience, this is where most physicians are behind the times. In the past, when adding a new member to a group, the new physician merely bought a portion of the assets of the practice and financed the build-up of his or her own receivables. Goodwill generally was not charged to the new member. Likewise, a retiring or leaving physician received only his share of the assets plus his accounts receivable.

When valuing a group, the first thing I analyze is the partnership or group ownership agreement, if any. Most of them are out of date and do not reflect current realities. For example, in one very successful internal medicine group a retiring physician received only the depreciated book value for equipment assets plus the physician's accounts receivable. The retiring doctor was short-changed the value of the goodwill, which in this instance was significant. The new doctor entering the group did not have to pay anything for the value of entering a successful group practice with an immediate full-time patient load.

An ENT group that I recently worked with had three members in an expense-sharing arrangement. They needed to add a fourth physician because of the rapidly increasing patient load and the desire of one of the physicians to cut back his practice in anticipation of retirement. The two younger physicians had joined the group a few years ago, again with no goodwill being charged. However, this group, because of its reputation and location, had considerable goodwill. Only after consid-erable input did all members of the group finally decide that there was a goodwill value for their individual practices. The new physician entered the arrangement by paying for a share of the physical assets, accounts receiv-able, plus about $90,000 to the original three physicians for goodwill. The new physician now has almost a full-time practice after only a few months in the clinic, plus a net income that is comparable to his specialty only after five to seven years of experience. In this instance, everyone came out ahead. I even had a long-distance telephone con-ference call with the new physician and the administrator of the hospital where he was completing his residency. The administrator wanted to learn more about valuing practices because the hospital was getting ready to buy some of the practices of its medical staff in order to protect its patient referral base.

If for no other reason than to protect your spouse in case of your untimely death, I always recommend that physicians in group practice review their group agreements. If the agreement is not updated, with a formula or system for valuing the leaving doctor's share of the practice, then the estate or family will be the losers. This also is true for disability. It is even more critical if you are disabled, since the income from the goodwill value of your practice could lessen considerably the impact of disability on your future income.

As a start, your group or clinic should have an appraisal done to determine the current value of each doctor's practice. Then, once a formula for using this value for a buy-in or buy-out has been completed, the group agreement and any employment contracts should be updated. When a member is added or deleted, an update of the appraisal can be completed to get the current value of the individual practice. For even better financial planning, key person insurance could be purchased to fund any buy-outs caused by death or disability. This would simplify the practice transfer without creating a financial hardship on remaining group members. Otherwise, a new physician would have to be recruited to buy into the practice and provide the source of funds for the leaving doctor's funds.

All of this is a fairly recent phenomenon. Just as the clinical practice of medicine has changed drastically recently, so have the financial aspects of practice valuation. In this respect, dentists are a long way ahead of physicians, since their practices have had value for a longer time, and most dentists realize the importance of planning for this.

The facts back up this chapter's discussion on valuation. According to the Physician Recruiting Survey Results for 1984, from the Center for Research in Ambulatory Health Care Administration (*Medical World News*, August 14, 1987), over 70% of physicians joining a practice paid a buy-in cost when joining a group practice (Figure 11). Thirty-three percent paid $25,000 or more.

Figure 11

FACTS ON NEW PHYSICIANS
JOINING A GROUP PRACTICE

Approximate buy-in cost to new MD

No buy-in cost	29.5%
$5,000 or less	13.2%
$5,001-$25,000	23.3%
$25,001-$50,000	15.0%
$50,001 plus	18.8%

5

MAXIMIZING PRACTICE VALUATION

"The key to successful investing in the stock market is to buy low and sell high..."

This same principle applies to a practice sale. In order to sell high, the practice must appear to be growing and successful. Dr. Older, our example from Chapter One, let his practice dwindle until the value was almost nothing. Dr. Wiser had a successful practice sale because he planned ahead and made changes to enhance the practice value. Thus, the purpose of this chapter is to help you, the seller, to maximize the market value of your practice. This also has significant benefit for the buyer. A growing, successful practice may cost more, but may be an astute investment in terms of future income for the buyer.

WHAT ARE THE ELEMENTS OF A SUCCESSFUL SALE?

To understand how to maximize practice value, you need to know the basic elements of a practice sale and how they can be enhanced to increase value or the likelihood of a successful sale. These elements are shown in Figure 12.

Figure 12

ELEMENTS OF A SUCCESSFUL SALE

Plan ahead
Establish a fair market value
Maintain an active patient flow
Select the right buyer or associate
Complete all documentation
Insure an effective changeover
Leave the practice

The first element, planning ahead, is critical. Unless your particular circumstances preclude this, planning ahead will be the most effective technique to receive maximum value and price for the practice. Reading this book is the first stage of the planning process. The second stage is taking the time to make changes. Without taking this time, changes will not be implemented. Therefore, if there are serious problems with your practice, the sale process should be postponed until these problems can be addressed.

After you have established a fair market value for the practice, take some time to reflect on what this means. If the appraisal was done so that positives and negatives about the practice were identified, consider these and decide if additional action is necessary before accepting the appraisal. If your practice has none or only a few minor problems, these should not interfere with the completion of the sale process. However, if concrete problems are identified, two things may occur. First, the appraisal is probably on the low side, since the problems were discounted in the practice market value estimate. Second, buyers may discount the practice even more. This will make it doubly difficult to get the best price for your practice.

If the problems can be addressed and solved, have the practice reappraised. The investment of your time and money in the practice changes should pay off with a higher appraisal and a greater likelihood of getting the appraisal price from a buyer. If it is not possible to make changes, accept the fact that you probably will not get the appraisal value and that the sale process may be more difficult because you will be on the defensive in the negotiations.

The next step is to maintain an active patient flow. This is the major reason that someone will buy a professional practice. There are several ways of doing this. An active recall system, if your practice is geared towards this clinically, will maintain the patient flow. Combining this with encouraging current patients to refer new patients should be all that is necessary to keep the practice active and growing. Try to keep a good mix of age groups in the practice; most buyers are younger and they usually prefer young families as patients.

For subspecialists, priming of the referral network pump is a good strategy. Try to keep the referral base growing. If all of your referring colleagues are older, they also may be retiring soon, and this will detract from the practice value. New blood in the referral network will keep it healthy.

Selecting the right buyer or associate is the major decision during the sale process. In my experience, it is important to establish a personality fit between buyer and seller before going on further in the process. Once this has been done, then other factors can be evaluated, such as clinical expertise and financial background. Since much of the practice sale price may be unsecured, the future success is based on a judgment of how successful the new buyer will be.

All documentation should be completed before the sale can be considered final. For example, earnest money agreements, sale contracts, installment notes, lien filings, and financial terms need to be documented, agreed to and signed before the new buyer takes over or joins the practice.

The estate of a doctor lost a lot of money because final contracts were not signed before the new doctor took over. He then changed his mind about the practice, found an excuse to break off negotiations, and basically ruined the practice for anyone else. This could easily have been avoided if all documentation had been completed before the practice was transferred.

To insure an effective changeover, every part of the practice sale process must be designed to enhance patient flow. For example, be sure that no staffing changes are made immediately, as this can upset patients. Do not change location or telephone number. Even leaving your name on the door for a reasonable time period is a good idea. Continuity of care must be maintained. Patients will be apprehensive about a new person taking over the practice; thus, gear all communication to emphasize the clinical and personal skills of the new buyer, your confidence in that person, and your confidence in the future.

Finally, it is important emotionally to leave the practice. Interference from a former owner can disrupt even the best strategy for a successful practice sale.

An overview of the entire sale process has just been completed. Subsequent chapters will explore in more detail the elements outlined above. However, for purposes of maximizing value, the overview indicates one consistent theme—presenting the practice, yourself, and the success of the practice in the best possible light. If your practice is presented well, the maximum price will be obtained.

This presentation starts immediately when first talking to a potential buyer. When meeting a buyer, treat that person as you would a patient during a treatment presentation. Your goal is to create the idea in the buyer's mind that the practice is the best for his or her needs.

DO PEOPLE REALLY JUDGE A BOOK BY ITS COVER?

Your mother probably has drilled this pearl of wisdom into your brain. Mothers also like to say "Beauty is only skin deep." However, what is reality? A patient's first impressions of you and your office are critical. Most of us make judgments about others within the first four minutes of contact. These first impressions are lasting ones, and can determine whether or not a patient stays with the practice and refers other patients to the practice.

Dr. George Bach's research (*Contact: The First Four Minutes*, Zunin, pg. 25) concludes that, "Mainly, one thinks of others as one did on first meeting them. Initial illusions tend to be preserved." Real estate personnel recommend painting a house inside and out before putting it on the market. Lawns should be recently mowed, landscaping completed, and even fresh flowers in windows are helpful. All of this creates an image in the buyer's mind before entering the house.

In less time than it takes to say hello, a personnel manager will judge an applicant's poise; how he or she stands and speaks; how the clothes appear, whether they fit, and whether they are neat and appropriate. If negative, the job interview probably will be fruitless for the applicant.

First impressions may not always be correct, but they are a fact of life. For example, a conservative dresser will instill confidence. A slick dresser makes us look for a gimmick. A beautiful person is considered to be kind, sympathetic and energetic. Also, people tend to classify others based on initial impressions—socioeconomic category, wealth, education and importance. Thus, quicker than the blink of an eyelid, your initial contact with a new buyer may be doomed because of a poor first impression.

Real estate personnel also know that most sales are made by the time the buyer opens the door and walks into the house. Use the same strategy with your practice.

I have been in hundreds of medical and dental offices. By the time I have opened the front door and walked across the reception room to greet the receptionist, I can predict the gross revenue of the practice, the doctor's net income and the staff's morale. All of this comes from a sixth sense that is triggered by the ambience of the office. It is surprising how close these guesses are. Since I can validate my estimate based upon actual financial information and staff input about the practice, this sixth sense has been honed to precision.

When I am wrong, I usually estimate that the practice is less successful than it really is. Why? The doctor's success does not come across in the initial impression that the office itself gives off.

The good news is that a positive initial impression tends to build upon itself if it gets reinforcement throughout the practice sale cycle. This greatly simplifies the practice sale and enhances the likelihood of receiving top price for the practice.

I have one more example of how initial impressions can enhance practice value. When consulting or when teaching residents, many clients and students will ask if wearing a tie while seeing patients is important (for men, that is). I always answer by quoting the following experiment by the dress for success advocate John T. Malloy (*Class*, Paul Fussell, 1983, pg. 67):

> Malloy posed as a middle-class man who had left his wallet and somehow needed to get back to his home in the suburbs. During rush hour at the Port Authority Bus Terminal in New York, he tried to borrow 75 cents for his bus fare. The first hour he wore a suit but no tie, the second hour he was properly dressed, tie and all. "In my first hour I made $7.23. However, in the second hour, with my tie on, I made $26.00, and one man even gave me extra money for a newspaper."

Malloy's experiment has even more importance for a practice sale. Instead of a few dollars, though, we are talking about tens of thousands of dollars.

When giving a talk or seminar, I always wear a nice suit, put on a freshly laundered shirt, and make sure that my hair is combed and my grooming impeccable. Why? Research indicates that an audience judges a speaker 60% on appearance, 20% on manner and only 20% on content. Thus, even though I consider the content of my talks to be the most important part of the process, I also know that a favorable initial reaction by the audience insures they will listen in a positive manner to what is being said. It enhances the communication process. If I wore my jogging outfit, or my western riding clothes, the audience naturally would question my capabilities in practice management and practice selling.

For example, wearing a cowboy hat, I probably could talk about investing in pork belly futures and get away with it. However, I have never bought a futures contract nor seen a pig's belly.

In a nutshell, take a look at your practice sometime from the front door, not through the private back entrance. You may be surprised at what you see. Look at your practice as a potential buyer or new patient would—and make sure that the initial impression is positive. It makes the rest of the sale process go much smoother and can result in financial gain.

To put this in perspective, let's examine the importance of initial impressions on your *own* patients. Buyers also should pay close attention to this section, as future practice growth will be dependent upon the success buyers have with new patients.

First, examine the patient contact cycle. This is shown in Figure 13. The patient contact cycle is eight different phases a new patient goes through when visiting a doctor's office. Each contact phase is an initial impression created in the patient's mind. As each phase is examined, think about your own practice and how it stacks up against the "perfect" practice. Remember, this is to learn about your own practice, and the impact it will have on a potential buyer. As a corollary benefit, it may even improve your present practice if changes are implemented based upon accurate observations.

A new patient's (buyer's) initial contact with you may be from a listing in the Yellow Pages, an advertisement, a chance meeting with you or a staff member, your office brochure, as a walk-in off the street, or as a referral from a colleague, friend or patient. All these sources of initial contact must be professional and enhance the credibility of the practice.

Figure 13
PATIENT CONTACT CYCLE

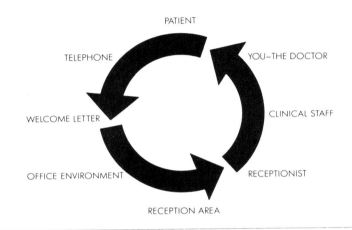

The next contact usually is the *telephone* —to make an appointment or to get information about the practice. The way the phone call is answered is also critical. If the voice is friendly, warm and helpful, the patient has a positive impression. If the patient gets a busy signal, is put on hold, or is handled in a curt or defensive manner, the initial impression obviously is negative. Say goodby to that new patient. Many local telephone companies offer inexpensive telephone image seminars. They can be an excellent investment for you and your staff.

Next, the patient sees the outside of the *office*. If the office is easy to locate, if parking is readily available, if the outside environment is safe, if the ease of access to the building is good, if the elevator or stairway is clean, and if the office door invites the patient to come in, then the patient should be positively impressed.

Next, the patient sees the *reception room*. The reception area is probably the most important non-verbal communication to the patient in his assessment of the practice. If the office looks clean and up-to-date, the patient automatically will assume that your treatment will reflect these same qualities.

The reception area should create a feeling of high trust and low fear. Ideally, the reception area should evoke a sense of understated class. Patients want to be treated by successful practitioners; this is reflected immediately in the reception area. The key is to make it modern, comfortable and warm, but not ostentatious. This implies a quiet elegance. The days of linoleum floors, 1950s vinyl furniture, and plastic flowers are over. If the reception area has a dirty or untidy appearance, what do you think will be in the patient's mind concerning the quality of your skills?

The next contact is the *receptionist*. This is probably the first face-to-face meeting the patient will have with the staff. A friendly, attentive, and helpful receptionist will insure a positive impression. However, if the receptionist is curt, and the patient feels that he is being treated like a number, a negative impression results. Personal attention is the key. Next in line will be the *clinical staff*. From greeting the patient in the reception room to casual talk in the exam room, the staff's goal should be to let the patient know the staff is committed to excellent health care. Their appearance and attitude should reflect excellence and professionalism.

Again, personal attention is the key. If the staff can put themselves in the patient's position, they can develop the empathy necessary to make the patient feel comfortable and wanted. The staff should pronounce the name of the patient correctly, act in a friendly and helpful manner, and keep the patient calm during this introductory phase of the visit.

The appearance of the exam room should be comfortable, up-to-date, clean, neat, and non-threatening to the patient.

Finally, the patient gets to see you, the *doctor.* After several initial impressions, the final image of the practice is solidly entrenched in the patient's mind. If this image is positive, you can reinforce that image, and it would take a lot of errors on your part to make it negative. Contrary to what most doctors believe, the patient's impression of you will not be based upon the technical quality of your clinical skills, but more on how you come across to the patient as a *person.* If the patient's initial impressions so far through this cycle are negative, all the money you have spent for overhead probably is wasted. At the very least, you will need all of your people skills to turn this patient around.

As you can see, looking at your practice from the eyes of a new patient basically is the same process that a new buyer will go through. However, a new buyer may be even more critical of flaws seen during the initial contact cycle. If the buyer is turned off at the beginning, receiving a price for the practice, or even an offer itself, that is close to the market value may be difficult.

Even appraisers may be subject to the same "initial impression syndrome." Your appraisal probably will be higher if the appraiser initially is impressed visually with the practice. This is a subconscious reaction, but a proper one.

The patient interaction cycle is now complete. Remember, everything you do either reinforces or detracts from the image you are trying to get across to the patient or potential buyer. How do people perceive you? What are you telling them with your facility, reception room, staff, voice, actions, dress and manner?

SHOULD I UPGRADE MY EQUIPMENT AND FURNITURE?

Many professionals keep outdated or useless equipment, furniture, and supplies in their offices. In addition, the latest equipment may not be purchased because the physician is close to retirement and does not want to spend the time needed for training or improving skills. Worn reception room furniture and carpets may not be replaced. These are many of the mistakes that doctors make in order to save money or time before retiring or selling a practice. Again, remember that initial impressions are critical. Keep the practice assets up-to-date and visually appealing. The buyer probably will be younger and will not want to use an outdated instrument which he or she only has seen in old textbook photographs.

Recently, I sold the practice of a doctor who died of a sudden heart attack. His office was located on the second floor of an office building built in the 1940s and not remodeled since. There was no elevator, instead, there was the longest flight of stairs that I have seen outside of Washington, D.C. The doctor was in his sixties, and many of his patients were elderly. They probably stayed healthy just from the exercise of walking up and down the steps! The equipment was old and outdated, and some of their functions were not even known to the younger doctors who looked at the practice. The practice was sold to a younger doctor about four blocks away, but most of the equipment was junked during the move. The estate received a cash offer close to the appraisal value, and in about two weeks the transaction was complete. However, the practice sold for less than it could have been worth, mainly because of the office location and the outmoded equipment.

A dental equipment company, in its publication *What to Look for When Buying Dental Equipment* (A-dec, Inc., 1985), poses some very basic questions you should ask yourself about your equipment. These same questions also apply to medical practices. They are as follows:

- Although the existing equipment still may be operating up to the original standards, does it perform to *today's* standards? If not, your productivity may be impaired.

- Does the existing equipment require excessive maintenance and continued costly service calls? If it does, you are losing productive hours in downtime . . . as well as money in repair costs.

- Does the existing equipment look up-to-date, thus reassuring your patients they are in the hands of a modern, efficient doctor? If not, your image may suffer.

In summary, if you are satisfied that your current equipment allows you to be as productive as you want to be, does not require excessive service calls, and reinforces a progressive, competent image, then the current equipment is performing well. If you see weaknesses in any of these areas, then some long, hard thought is required. Why? Because the new buyer most likely will be younger, recently out of school, and used to the newer techniques and equipment. The practice image, and possibly price, may suffer. A well thought out plan to replace some of the equipment may pay greater dividends in the future than to keep outmoded equipment in the practice.

Go through the practice and discard unused equipment, instruments and supplies. This might be an excellent time to donate these to a voluntary clinic or school. Besides possibly getting a tax deduction, the office will look less cluttered.

As a bottom line, well-maintained and clean equipment and instruments not only look better, they are appraised higher.

MY PRACTICE IS NOT GROWING. WHAT SHOULD I DO?

A common practice situation found with doctors who are getting ready to retire is that their practices have stopped growing, and even may be declining. For a new buyer, lack of practice growth is a red flag concerning the future success of the practice. A practice that is increasing in collections every year is valued higher than a static or declining practice.

There usually are sound reasons for a practice that is static or declining. These usually are related to the amount of time spent in the practice by the doctor, and perhaps the style of practice. What will scare a potential buyer, though, is the thought that the practice is declining because the doctor is driving away patients—which spells doom for the buyer. However, this situation rarely occurs; but the decline in collections must be addressed, and corrected if possible. If the buyer feels that there is a risk in buying the practice, it will make it difficult, if not impossible, to obtain a good price for the practice, or possibly even to sell it at all.

What are the most common reasons for a static or declining practice (excluding the doctor driving away patients)?

- With the present competitive environment for patients, even a practice that is doing everything right may be just holding its own.

- The fee schedule may not be current. If fees have not been raised for a long time, practice collections may be steady, but net income will be eroded due to the inflationary impact on expenses.

- The most common reason is spending less time in the practice. This is a natural reaction to approaching retirement. The practice has caught a case of the "dwindles." If this dwindling situation gets out of hand, the doctor may not have a practice to sell.

- Many subspecialists may have let their referral sources dwindle. Colleagues who refer probably are facing retirement, too, and with each retirement of a referring doctor, the practice declines.

- In some cases, the health of the doctor may be declining, and thus the doctor's interest and impact on the practice is suffering. This occurs many times when a spouse is suffering ill health.

HOW DO I MAINTAIN PRACTICE GROWTH?

If the practice is not growing, a few steps can be taken to turn the practice around. These steps are referred to as "practice marketing." Many of you probably are recoiling in horror thinking about having to advertise for patients, since this is what the word "marketing" connotes to many doctors. However, marketing simply is making current patients satisfied with the practice so they will refer their

friends and acquaintances to the office. The encouragement of these referrals can be done easily in any office, and
in a professional and ethical manner. Advertising is not
required to accomplish this result.

If, after reading the recommendations for increasing
patient growth, you still do not want to implement the
suggestions, then accept this fact. However, it must be
communicated to the potential buyer in a manner that will
allay his or her fears about the future risk of the practice.
Being up front will temper the negative aspects of the
situation. Inform the potential buyer that you are unable to
increase practice growth due to whatever reason is appropriate. For example, you have decided to practice only
three days a week in order to prepare for retirement; your
health has been declining and you have had to limit the
time in the office; or your spouse has been in ill health and
requires more of your time and energy.

The following suggestions are from my book *Marketing:
For Practice Growth* (HELP Publications, 1985). The most
important aspect of practice marketing is that current
patients be satisfied with the practice. If they are, they will
refer new patients. These referrals are responsible, in the
average primary care practice, for 60 to 70% of all new
patients. Most of these suggestions are only common
sense, but they still get results.

- Make your patients aware that you appreciate new
  patient referrals. Many patients think some doctors
  do not accept new patients. This is a carryover from
  the early days when all a doctor had to do was to hang
  up a shingle and watch the patients come in.

- Put out information in the reception room magazine

rack, bulletin boards, and on the walls of the reception area indicating your background, your clinical skills and that you accept new patient referrals.

- Post a sign at the reception desk where patients check in and check out, stating that new patient referrals are encouraged.

- Indicate in the practice brochure that you encourage new patient referrals.

- Ask who referred the patient on the New Patient Information form. The receptionist should comment on it to the patient, and you also should reinforce it when first meeting the new patient. For example, say "We really like referrals. It was nice of Mrs. Jones to refer you to our practice."

- Thank current patients for referrals. Dale Carnegie once said, "People tend to repeat those actions for which they have been shown appreciation." A thank you can take the form of a simple hand-written note to the current patient thanking him or her for the referral. If you like, after multiple referrals, you may send a bouquet of flowers to the patient's place of employment as a very effective attention-getter and thank you. It gets the attention not only of the patient, but also of the rest of the staff in the office. Other gifts that are effective include a gift certificate for dinner at a local restaurant, or tickets to a theater.

- Statement stuffer can indicate acceptance of referrals.

- If you send out patient newsletters, include articles on how patient referrals have helped the practice and your thanks to your current patients for referrals.

WHAT ELSE CAN BE DONE TO INCREASE PRACTICE GROWTH?

Recognizing patient achievements is another practice-builder. People like to be noticed, recognized, and complimented on their achievements. It reinforces their own sense of identity and striving. Also, showing patients that you care when significant events happen in their lives is a good patient ego-booster. People remember compliments and acts of caring. They often are surprised that their doctor thinks of them as human beings with feelings. They reward these acts with positive feelings about you and your staff, and are more likely to tell their friends about you.

Some methods to recognize patient achievements and life events are as follows:

- Have the staff regularly scan the newspaper for articles about the patients. Either clip the article and send it to the patient, put it in the patient's chart and mention it the next time the patient comes into the office, or put it on the bulletin board.

- If the patient is in the hospital, send him a get well card or a basket of fruit. The card should be personally signed by you and/or the staff.

- Record patients' birthdays and anniversaries on the computer, or use a system similar to the recall system, and send the patients greeting cards on their birthdays or anniversaries.

- You may want to send patients Christmas or holiday cards as well.

- Offer small gifts at time of service. These are usually inexpensive, but can be very effective in thanking the patient for the visit and having the patient think well of you. Examples are magnets, bandaids, children's items such as rings, posters, sugarless candy, personalized pens or pencils, or personalized balloons.

- Give the patient a telephone sticker noting emergency numbers for the police, fire department, hospital, dentist and physician.

CAN THE STAFF HELP IN INCREASING PATIENT REFERRALS?

Yes, the staff can be a very effective referral service. To encourage their referrals, make it easy for them to refer friends and acquaintances and reward their actions. The following ideas can aid in this effort:

- Staff business cards can be very helpful as a referral booster. Have them printed and encourage the staff to hand them out when making financial arrangements, for post-treatment instructions, and to their friends and relatives in order to make them aware of where the staff person works. Business cards also give the staff a sense of identity with the practice.

- After a member of the staff has referred a number of new patients (perhaps five), offer a gift certificate from a prestigious department store. This can be a very effective reward system.

- You may want to plan a nice dinner for the staff and their spouses when a major practice goal for new patient referrals has been met.

In summary, encouraging new patient referrals from current patients is a simple process. What it takes is a critical awareness that you accept new patients and that you encourage new patient referrals. Solid motivators such as sending thank you notes and recognizing patient achievements will show that you care for the patient as a person, and will make the patient comfortable in referring other patients to the practice. Do not forget the staff. Reward them generously when they refer patients, and they will take a much more active interest in the success of the practice.

For example, one client, after having an appraisal, decided to grow his practice for a couple of years through the above marketing techniques. A buyer was then found for the practice, but the client was so satisfied with the way things were now going that he decided to postpone retirement. Who knows; this could even happen to you.

WHAT ABOUT ALTERNATE DELIVERY SYSTEMS?

In the past, doctors built their practices through fee-for-service patients. Now, capitation plans, Preferred Provider Organizations (PPOs) and Health Maintenance Organizations (HMOs) must be considered. These alternative delivery systems are becoming very important to doctors, and need to be considered in overall practice growth strategy.

Capitation is a system in which a doctor contracts to assume the financial risk for patient care. Compensation is based on a predetermined rate per patient or family. Patients can utilize only the services of member doctors.

Preferred Provider Organizations cover a broad spectrum of health care providers, insurance companies and businesses. A doctor usually contracts directly with the

PPO and agrees to a discounted fee schedule in return for access to a larger group of potential patients.

Health Maintenance Organizations provide comprehensive health care benefits at little or no out-of-pocket expense to the insured. The premiums paid finance a *closed* system of individual and institutional providers.

Capitation plans, PPOs and HMOs should be included in practice planning. However, the main point to keep in mind is that each system basically asks you to provide health care at a discount to normal fees. Thus, the final decision should be based on a *very thorough* analysis of the bottom line financial impact a proposed system will have on the total practice. The critical factor is that most of these are closed systems. If you do not join the organization, will you lose current patients who can no longer see you for care? By not joining, you may hurt the future of the practice, and thus decrease its value to a buyer.

I must emphasize again that this can be a critical financial decision. One of my clients called to ask what impact his joining a capitation plan would have on his practice value. He would be seeing, potentially, about one thousand new patients. An associate probably would need to be hired, along with more staff. I asked him what impact the plan would have on his net income. He did not know! The reimbursement schedule was not fully established. I told him that if his net income went up, his practice value probably would increase. On the other hand, if his net income went down, the practice value would decrease, and even the future of the practice might be in jeopardy. Obviously, a very thorough analysis must be done before taking action. Talk to colleagues, state societies, an attorney, accountant or other sources. Do not rely on the insurance company salesperson, as his or her goals are not the same as yours.

HOW DOES A SUBSPECIALIST INCREASE PRACTICE GROWTH?

The need for referrals from primary care doctors varies depending on what the subspecialty is and how long the doctor has practiced. For example, a surgeon will probably get 90% of referrals from other doctors, and not from current patients. On the other hand, an OB/GYN may receive less than 50% of new patient referrals from other doctors. However, no matter what the subspecialty, a constant flow of new patients is needed.

When a doctor refers to a subspecialist, what is he or she looking for?

- A subspecialist who has a good personality in terms of dealing with patients.

- A subspecialist with excellent clinical skills. The referring doctor needs to have faith in the subspecialist's clinical ability to handle patient problems. This is the one area where clinical skills are important because they can be assessed by the referring doctor. If you are good, referrals will grow. If you are not clinically skilled, eventually it will catch up with you in terms of decreased referrals.

I am assuming that you are clinically current and have a good patient personality. Even with these attributes, you may find patient referrals have dropped off. The primary reason is probably that you have not kept the referral network replenished with new doctors as others have left practice or found other subspecialists. In order to increase the size of the network, make frequent contact with them.

The key concept to keep in mind when developing professional referrals is the following:

"OUT OF SIGHT, OUT OF MIND"

What can you do to increase your visibility and encourage new referrals?

- Personal visits are the most important in terms of developing referrals. Going to the offices of primary care doctors and talking with them face to face is very effective.

- Written communications, consisting of clinical results letters, referral thank you letters, and patient release letters, increase visibility. Telephone calls also can be a good practice builder, followed by written communication.

- Give seminars to small groups of doctors, explaining your specialty and guidelines for diagnoses for referrals to you.

- Society involvement is also important. You may want to talk at general meetings, get involved on committees, and with community and social activities of the society. This way you come into contact with a large number of doctors.

- Social contacts strengthen and increase referral probabilities. Select activities that you enjoy; otherwise your insincerity will come across.

- Send reprints of any clinical journal articles you have written, or feel would be of interest, to primary care doctors.

■ Remember referral sources during holidays, birthdays, or other significant personal events.

■ Meet the staff of colleagues. Get to know them on a one-on-one basis. Introduce your own staff to them. This will help keep your name at the top of the referral list, and if problems should ever occur, will help to surmount them.

■ If you are located close to a medical school, then teaching can expose you to graduating doctors. Since the majority of doctors practice close to their schools after residency, you will be the obvious choice for referrals. Teaching also adds credibility to your background. In addition, the staff at school clinics can be an invaluable source of referrals.

■ Make yourself available to colleagues. Work in emergency or rush appointments as soon as possible. Call back immediately when a referring doctor calls you. Train the staff to respond to the V.I.P.s of the practice.

What if the doctor you are contacting already has referral subspecialists lined up? The solution is to break into the referral network. This can be done by offering to become a "second source" for the doctor in case his or her primary source is out of town, or an emergency has come up and the primary source is not available. Once you have been able to break down this barrier, do all within your power to insure that any referred patients are successfully treated and that this is communicated to the referring doctor.

One group of subspecialists asked me how to increase their referrals from younger doctors. I told them to invite one of the younger doctors to their meetings, and have him talk to them about what younger colleagues are looking for when they choose a referral subspecialist. Just this exposure may open up some doors to the older subspecialists.

As a wrap-up to this section on marketing, remember times are changing. As one client told me, in reference to the competitive environment health care is finding itself in, "It's a battle zone out there!" Most wars are won by a series of small battles and skirmishes. Eventually the tide turns and the battle is won. Take care of the details of marketing your practice, and you will be the victor.

It is time to shift gears and look at one of the most critical variables in maximizing practice value—net income.

WHY IS PRACTICE NET INCOME A CRITICAL VARIABLE?

In determining goodwill valuation, practice net income is the biggest factor. The higher the net income, the more money a buyer will have to pay off any practice note or bank loan. The example given earlier in the book showed how net income could have a $60,000 impact on the valuation of goodwill for two "identical" practices.

The average net income percentage for primary care medical practices is in the 50% range (net income as a percentage of collections). For subspecialty surgical practices, net income may average as high as 65%. For dental practices, the average net income is about 40% of collections.

During the appraisal, it is important to remove some expense items from the calculation. For example, if the practice is incorporated, remove the officer's salary from the expense category. The same is true for personal and employee retirement plan contributions and interest on practice loans. A buyer may not want a retirement plan, and he or she will have their own interest payments based upon the buy-out. In my appraisals I also delete depreciation, as this is a non-cash expense. By doing all of these calculations, it is possible to compare various practices on an equal basis statistically.

If you own the building, then a rent adjustment factor needs to be calculated. In most cases, the building is sold to the new buyer. However, if this will not be happening, expenses may be understated because no rent has been factored into the new buyer's expense profile. Deduct mortgage interest, property taxes and other building ownership costs from expenses, then add in a reasonable rent figure.

WHAT IF MY NET INCOME IS LOWER THAN AVERAGE?

If the net income percentage is low, the most common reason is excess staffing costs. Primary care doctors should have an average payroll cost (salaries, payroll taxes and benefits) which amounts to 20 to 25% of collections. Invariably, in low net income practices, this percentage is much higher.

What can be done to lower payroll costs? This is a very difficult situation in most instances. If the staff has little turnover, then staffing salaries naturally will increase above average due to annual increases. However, staff turnover is a negative for evaluating goodwill. This out of balance situation probably will correct itself over time as staff members retire or make job changes.

What is more likely to be the case is that the practice is

overstaffed. Temporary employees end up becoming part-time, then full-time employees. Another employee is hired on a temporary basis and the cycle repeats itself. If overstaffing is the problem, some hard decisions will have to be made. I have found, when doing practice overhead analysis consulting, that most staff members realize they are not busy enough to justify all the positions that are filled. Therefore, once the decision has been made to reduce staffing costs, the implementation action already has been surmised by the staff, and proceeds uneventfully.

Sometimes family members are included in office payroll for services that may not be utilized by the new buyer. Thus, this can be eliminated from expenses.

Perhaps the practice can become more efficient, for example by utilizing computer timeshare billing instead of hand ledger card billing. This is especially helpful with insurance forms. The staff savings should be more than the increased cost of an outside billing service. There also will be better practice control of accounts receivable.

Other areas of expense may need to be analyzed. For tax purposes, most practices try to include as much as possible in the expense category in order to reduce taxable income. Ideally, practice net income would be zero. Therefore, some practices need a line-by-line analysis of expense items. A pro forma expense projection, for the new buyer, should be made. For example, travel and continuing education expenses may include lease payments for the new Mercedes, trips to Hawaii for meetings, or use of the beach condo as a satellite office.

Professional services may include legal and accounting expenses related to the upgrading of the retirement plan or other non-recurring special situations. A revised, realistic expense profile for the new buyer may result in a more normal practice overhead situation.

WHAT IF MY NET INCOME PERCENTAGE IS HIGH?

If net income percentage is very high, then additional expenses may need to be added back, in order to give the buyer a true assessment of the costs. Common areas include no allowance for rent if the seller owns the building, and deflated staffing costs because a spouse or other relative is on the staff with a very small or no salary.

As explained earlier, it is a good idea to point out reasons for high or low overhead expenses. This will help the appraiser and the potential buyer to do a better job of analyzing the practice. This is another good reason for planning ahead, especially if you are able to impact on the net income percentage by making changes now in the practice.

WHAT IMPACT CAN ACCOUNTS RECEIVABLE HAVE ON PRACTICE VALUE?

Accounts receivable usually are not included in the practice buy-out. The seller generally arranges for them to be collected by the buyer and turned over to the seller. Therefore, the value of accounts receivable does not impact directly on the value of the practice. However, accounts receivable can have a subtle impact on the practice sale price and the ease of selling.

Accounts receivable are a direct measure of the quality of management of the practice. For example, accounts receivable that are higher than normal can indicate that collections are not being made in an efficient manner. Accounts receivable that have a high percentage of past due accounts (over 120 days) also indicate management deficiencies. Buyers will notice this, and question the quality of the practice management style.

How can you tell if accounts receivable are too high? Merely divide the receivables by the average production for the past few months. For example, if production is at the rate of $20,000 per month, and receivables are $60,000, then the ratio of accounts receivable to monthly production is 3.0 ($60,000 divided by $20,000 = 3.0). Thus, three months of production is tied up in receivables. Another way to look at this number is to say that if you produce $1.00 today, it will not be collected for three months.

For a well-managed practice, accounts receivable, stated as the number of months of average production, will be in the range of two and one-half to three and one-half months. If the ratio is higher than three and one-half months, then serious collection problems may be present. If the practice is on a cash basis (collecting at time of service), then receivables naturally should be less than two and one-half months.

Why is average monthly production, and not average monthly cash collections, used to calculate the receivables ratio? This is because if the practice suddenly grows rapidly, then receivables temporarily will increase quickly due to the lag time from billing to collecting. Conversely, if time has been taken off for a three-month sabbatical, then receivables will have dropped to an artificial low. Using monthly production evens out these potential blips.

A high accounts receivable may not necessarily indicate poor financial management. Many doctors do not write off uncollectible accounts, but leave them on the books forever. Therefore, an accurate value for accounts receivable needs to be determined. Another ratio to consider is the percentage of accounts receivable over 120 days old. For an average practice, this should be less than 40%. For example, if receivables are $50,000, and $20,000 has not been collected for at least 120 days, the ratio is 40% ($20,000 divided by $50,000). If the ratio is greater than 40%, examine individual accounts. If they cannot be collected, write them off, send them to collection, or do anything to get them out of the system. Cleaning out these old accounts will result in a true picture of receivables, and thus of the quality of the practice management.

In summary, taking the steps described in this chapter will help to maximize practice valuation and make the practice easier to sell. The first step is to enhance the initial impression of the practice. After that, concentrate on maintaining practice growth. Then make changes in specific areas that will increase practice net income and other practice financial ratios. All of this work will pay off in a higher price and quicker sale for the practice.

6

FINDING THE RIGHT BUYER OR ASSOCIATE

"There's something to talk up about the most ramshackle place. The other day a minuscule home came on the market. It is not important if I like it personally. This house is perfect for a young couple just starting out. Every home has a buyer. The trick is finding him."

This is a quote from an article in *Success* (November, 1987, pg. 53). As Nicholas Barsan, reportedly the most successful real estate salesperson in the country, indicates, the trick is finding the right buyer. Just as a health care practice will not function without patients, a practice will not sell without a buyer. Identifying and locating potential buyers generates significant anxiety for sellers.

Finding the right buyer is critical. The success of the practice sale depends upon judgment in selecting the right person. Almost every doctor getting ready to sell a practice experiences a queasy feeling in the pit of his stomach, thinking "What if I get my practice back?" This is not a happy thought.

I tried, for this book, to interview a doctor who had to take his practice back one year after the sale. His response was that he did not want to talk about it. As a matter of fact, he could not even discuss the topic. Obviously, the hurt and pain were too much to deal with. Actually, it happens so infrequently that it is not a major concern, but every step in the practice sale process must be followed closely to minimize the danger.

Questions clients and participants in seminars frequently ask are:

- Where will I find a buyer?
- How will I know he or she will be good with my patients?
- Where will the money come from?
- How do I respond to price questions?
- How do I keep it confidential?

There are many ways to reduce this anxiety level. The first thing to realize is that the process may take three months or up to two years, but a buyer *will be found*. Sometimes the eventual buyer comes from a totally unexpected source. Therefore, take as many steps as you can to open up the field for potential purchasers.

WHAT ARE THE STEPS INVOLVED IN COMPLETING A SALE?

The most common successful practice changeovers involve the process shown in Figure 14.

The remainder of the book will concentrate on walking through each one of these practice sale steps. Each step is

Figure 14
PRACTICE SALE PROCESS

Identifying and locating potential buyers
Selecting the best potential buyers for follow-up
Interviewing and showing the practice
Negotiating the initial sale price and terms
Obtaining an earnest money agreement
Accepting an offer
Arranging financing
Finalizing the sales contracts and allocations
Closing the sale
Initiating transitional tasks

necessary, and must be completed before moving on to the next stage.

Before proceeding, a review is necessary. The previous chapters have covered the foundation required to get a practice ready for sale. A reason for selling has been identified, a strategy prepared, and an appraisal has been completed.

If the appraisal indicates that the practice is in tip-top shape, then the time is right to begin the sale process. However, if the appraisal indicates some areas that are negative in terms of total practice value and if your timing permits it, you may want to spend a few months, or even years, upgrading the practice per the suggestions in the previous chapter. Try to determine which upgrades will have the most impact on practice value and proceed from there.

If timing and reasons for selling do not allow any room for changes, recognize that fact and proceed with the sale process. It is very important to be up front with potential buyers. By admitting potential negatives ahead of time and implying that the appraisal already reflects these consider- ations, you will be in a stronger negotiating stance later.

It is not necessary to bare your soul about every aspect of the practice. Something you consider to be a negative may not have the same impact on another professional. However, by taking the wind out of prospective buyers' attempts to reduce the price, the end result will be more financially beneficial to you.

WHAT IS A NATURAL BUYER?

One source of potential buyers for a practice is called the natural buyer. The natural buyer will gain the most from purchasing the practice. A natural buyer usually will insure a smooth and successful completion of the practice sale. Some examples of natural buyers are as follows:

- An associate or employee who is now, or has been, involved with the practice. This person already knows the patients, staff and referral sources.

- For many medical practices, a hospital becomes a natural buyer. Many of our clients are hospitals who purchase medical practices to protect their own referral sources. One recent survey indicated that 20% of hospitals interviewed reported having pur- chased at least one physician's practice.

- A student who is from the geographic area and who will be graduating soon is also a natural buyer. Many return to their hometowns to set up practice.

■ A colleague in the building, or close by, may be looking to expand his or her practice. Selling the practice to someone down the hall can be very beneficial to both of you. The patients are used to the location, even if the practice is moved to the buyer's office. This may have some negatives, since some equipment and instruments may be surplus, as well as some of the staff. However, these potential problems can be addressed and probably solved to everyone's benefit.

■ One of your children or a relative may be the buyer. This is about as natural as you can get. If this is the case, it is even more important to structure the sale as a normal business transaction, and every step should be followed carefully. You do not want a problem with the transfer of the practice to impact your personal future interaction with the buyer.

WHAT ARE SOME OTHER SOURCES OF BUYERS?

If a natural buyer cannot be found, then the potential sources need to be expanded. Other sources are as follows:

University Graduating Classes

■ Many graduates will practice in the state where they go to school. Contact the closest school, or schools, and let them know you are interested in selling. However, recent graduates may not be the best buyers. They generally have not had any real world experience, are heavily in debt, and are unsure about their future plans. In my experience, they are difficult to pin down and can go off on tangents. Occasionally, a few mature students will be good buyers, but usually the recent graduates need a year or two of practice experience to make concrete plans for their future.

School Alumni Departments

- This can be a rewarding area to investigate. For the reasons given above, potential referrals from the alumni department are more likely to be qualified buyers.

State and Component Societies

- Most state organizations have a professional relations department. A few even have organized buyer lists and offer other practice sales help.

National Societies

- Both the American Medical Association and the American Dental Association have practice opportunities departments that list practices and refer potential buyers.

Equipment and Supply Dealers

- The detail person or equipment salesperson who routinely calls on you may be able to offer assistance. One national drug firm even has a free listing service. These people generally know the local market and can put you in touch with interested local buyers.

Colleagues

- If confidentiality is not a concern, then professional colleagues may be helpful. Let them know your plans. But be aware that it may be in *their* best interests that you *not* sell your practice, in order to minimize competition.

Practice Consultants and Brokers

- Practice consultants and brokers are the best source of potential buyers. Most spend considerable time and money developing lists of qualified buyers. Also, if confidentiality is critical, this may be the best route to follow.

- There are many national and local firms in the business. The most important selection criteria is to talk to doctors in your area who have used their services. Find out how much they charge, your obligations, and their success rate. Just as in real estate, a good broker or consultant usually is worth the cost in terms of your time, hassle, financial results, and expanding the potential purchaser pool.

All or some of the above sources can be utilized to find a potential buyer. As mentioned earlier, no one knows where the potential purchaser may come from. Therefore, use as broad an approach as possible, consistent with your confidentiality needs and personal time obligations, to expose the practice.

HOW CAN I ADVERTISE MY PRACTICE MYSELF?

If you are going to sell the practice yourself, then advertising probably will be essential. Most state and some component societies offer classified advertising for "Practice Opportunities" or "Practice for Sale." These usually are inexpensive, and confidentiality generally can be maintained. A P.O. Box reply will save time in prescreening potential buyers, but also may inhibit some responses. National society journals and publications also can be used, although these usually are more expensive.

If you are a subspecialist, the national society journals and publications are very important to use. These are read directly by your targeted buyer pool.

If you decide to run your own ad, keep in mind that only about 10% of the available practices actually are advertised. Most are sold through brokers or other advisers. Also, be aware of what the ad may be signalling to a potential buyer. By reading between the lines, the ad may give vital clues to a buyer, such as the following:

Established Practice: It is so old that it should have been closed down years ago.

Doctor Must Sell/Illness Forces Sale: The doctor is going bankrupt or is sick of private practice.

Financing Available: The doctor is desperate or the practice is way overpriced.

Terms Negotiable: Again, the doctor is desperate.

New Practice: If it just started, why sell it so quickly, unless the location is terrible?

Sportsman's Paradise: The practice probably is located in the middle of Yellowstone Park, and the nearest community is available only by dog sled.

A well-designed ad will attract the greatest number of qualified buyers. Ideally, the ad should provide the following three points of information:

- General type of practice
- Approximate size or gross
- Approximate location or geographical area

An ad by itself will not sell a practice. The purpose of the ad is to alert potential buyers that a practice may be available. The more information that is included in the ad, the less likely it is that qualified candidates will respond. Some part of the information about the practice may turn off the potential respondent. It is better to describe the practice in a more complete manner individually with the respondents. In this way, potential turnoffs can be addressed, and perhaps resolved based upon other aspects of the practice as a whole. Otherwise, the prospective buyer may turn off to the practice without seeing the entire picture.

I send practice descriptions to all residency training centers, medical and dental schools, alumni departments, and state and component society executives. This broad-based mailing program generates many leads. This same approach can be utilized yourself, or through a listing service. A listing service can save time, money and provide a better forum for the practice advertisement. Again, it is important to learn as much as possible about such a service before committing to it.

HOW DO I SELECT POTENTIAL BUYERS?

In most instances, the best buyers will be the ones you feel the most comfortable with in terms of personality and initial impression. Selecting the right buyer basically is a judgment call. Most doctors are concerned with how well the new person will treat their patients in the future, or fit in with their group practice partners. This is very legitimate, since you probably have spent the better part of your working life developing patient rapport and understanding. The right buyer will carry on this tradition and insure the continuing success of the practice. This is the bottom line for selecting the best buyer.

Pay attention to the initial impression that you get in telephone interviews, curriculum vitae readings, and face-to-face interviews. A sloppily written letter of introduction or CV is a red flag in terms of the professionalism and sincerity of the person. Hesitancy, aloofness, or difficulty in communicating with you also are potential problems. Think about how the person will communicate with patients.

Judging the clinical skills of the person is also important. This only can be done by you in a personal interview. You even may want to review some of your problem patients with the person to see how he or she would handle their cases. This can be very revealing and even may help in the future care of the patient.

Prescreening by telephone, curriculum vitae and mail must be done. On the average, for every six to seven respondents, only one potentially qualified buyer will emerge. You do not want to interrupt your office schedule or personal time doing face-to-face interviews with non-qualified people.

Many respondents only are curious about the size of the practice or how much you want to sell it for because they may want to sell their own practice. Time spent prescreening will pay off in terms of future time that will not be wasted. For example, I have had the following conversations with potential buyers:

> "I have just lost my medical license due to a problem with the hospital. Because of this I am declaring

bankruptcy next week. However, I would like to see some practices in Oregon and start practicing there as soon as possible."

"I just closed my private practice. I was really burned out from the long hours, on-call interruptions, cash flow problems and paperwork hassles. However, I would like to buy another practice."

"I left dentistry and started a restaurant. It went bankrupt and I had a nervous breakdown. However, now my analyst feels that I should go back into private practice. He thinks that I am ready to accept the challenges again. I'm not sure, but I might as well give it another try and see what happens. Can you show me some large practices?"

The buyer's timetable is a good indicator of how serious the buyer really is about purchasing the practice. If the person is not available for two years, and the need to sell the practice is now, there is not an immediate need to go further with that person. If the potential buyer cannot commit to a definite time frame, you probably are wasting time talking with that person. Psychologically, many potential buyers have the same problem that some doctors do when deciding to sell their practices—they cannot make up their minds. As discussed in the first chapter, FEAR, whether it is of buying or selling a practice, can freeze a person from making decisions.

Invite candidates who appear qualified to meet you in the office before or after patient hours or during lunch time. You do not want to interrupt patient scheduling. Also, this will let you concentrate on the person and not be interrupted by phone calls or patient/staff problems.

Do not disclose financial matters during the screening process, except for the approximate size of the practice.

What is needed at this time is to get a feeling for the person's personality, character, and clinical approach to patients.

However, it is important to determine the financial background of the candidates. This can be a simple question at this stage of the game, such as "How are you planning on paying for the practice?" The answer to that question usually will give enough information in order for the process to proceed. Do not be discouraged if the person indicates that they have no available cash. This is the norm. Most practices are financed with outside resources, and this will be discussed later. However, if the person is purposely vague or hesitant, then this can be a red flag to evaluate further before going on with the selection process.

I would like to address a topic that is occurring more often in practice sales—sexism. Most retiring doctors are male, because very few females entered this profession thirty years ago. Now women are increasing in the ranks of doctors. For example, in OB/GYN the ratio of female to male students is increasing rapidly. The same is true for family practice and internal medicine. The medical profession will soon be one-third female. For example, the *Annals of Internal Medicine*, July, 1987, published the following information (Figure 15):

Thus, from 1978 to 1998, the percentage of internal medicine graduates who are female will increase by almost 500%, from 6.6% to 36.9%.

Many selling doctors reject female candidates out of hand. This is a serious mistake. The most common excuse I hear is, "My patients will not come to a female doctor." Actually, this is the selling doctor's ego talking, not his brain. In reality, patients may even prefer a female doctor

Figure 15

**COMPOSITION OF ACTIVE INTERNIST
POPULATION, 1978; AND OF ENTRANTS
TO INTERNIST POPULATION, 1978–1998**

	1978	'78-83	'83-88	'88-93	'93-98
	Percentage				
Men	93.4	84.7	78.2	70.2	63.1
Women	6.6	15.3	21.8	29.8	36.9

over a male. Some of my most successful sales have been to female doctors. Therefore, try to separate your internal biases—whether sexual, racial, religious affiliation, or nationality—from the reality of patient acceptance.

For example, one male client rejected a female applicant, much to my surprise. The candidate was personable, well qualified, and obviously would be successful in the practice. The seller gave the following excuses:

> "The candidate does not seem serious and does not seem to want to work very hard." (She had been a nurse for ten years, and then had paid her own way through school!)

> "The candidate was not well-groomed." (She used minimal makeup, very effectively, and had a newer frizzled hair style, which was very attractive!)

> "The candidate may get married, have a baby, and quit the practice." (She was almost forty years old and had lived in the same city all of her life.)

On the other hand, occasionally I sell a female doctor's practice to a male doctor. It is interesting to notice the same fears arise when the female doctor is afraid that the male doctor will not be successful in her practice.

One important criteria, though, is communication ability. If the prospective buyer cannot communicate effectively in English with you, then he or she will not be able to communicate with your patients. This is an obvious negative.

You will want to check the person's references, credentials, school record, licensing status, and financial background. I usually recommend postponing this part of the selection process until it appears that the candidate is a serious buyer. A lot of time can be wasted checking out a person and then discovering that the person is left-handed and your equipment can be used only by a right-handed person. Thorough reference checking can wait. However, if the candidate has worked or gone to school with personal colleagues, then a quick call to them might pay off.

At this stage of the process the goal is to identify potential buyers, but not eliminate marginally acceptable ones, until more information is available. The candidate who appears marginal at first glance may have the staying power you are looking for in the practice. This is the first cut; next we have tryouts, and finally we select the ultimate team member.

7

NEGOTIATING SUCCESSFULLY

"I don't care what the final price is, it is the terms that count."

This sage advice was given to me by a very astute attorney. As you move through the negotiation part of the sale process, the appropriateness of this advice will become evident. Negotiating the final practice sale can be a quagmire—or it can be a period of mutual trust and understanding. Again, knowledge is the key. Knowledge can turn a process which can be full of pitfalls into a well-marked trail.

HOW DO I SHOW THE PRACTICE?

The last chapter discussed how to prescreen potential candidates and select those who have a good probability of success. The next step, showing the practice and interviewing the candidates in person, is a two-way street. As the seller, you are evaluating the potential purchaser and at the same time trying to present the practice in the best light to that person. It is important to keep these two aspects separate—at least in your own mind.

If you try too hard to present the practice, then concentration will be lost concerning your feelings about the person. On the other hand, subjecting the person to an interrogation may turn the person off to the purchase of the practice. It is best to concentrate first on the person, determine your interest in that person, and if positive, switch to the presentation of the practice itself.

Initial impressions again are critical. Make sure that the practice shows well. Pay attention to your initial reaction to the candidate. If both are positive, then the future will also be positive.

WHAT ARE SOME CRITERIA TO USE TO EVALUATE CANDIDATES?

The following are some suggested areas to use to evaluate potential candidates on a face-to-face basis:

Confident Attitude: This will be a positive indication of his or her clinical competence and ability to relate to patients.

Work Ethic: Is the candidate willing to work? Does this show up in the resume, or in activities engaged in during school?

Image: Does the candidate come across with a positive image in terms of appearance and personality?

Philosophy: Do you share the same views concerning patient care, continuing education and practice promotion?

Professional and Community Involvement: Candidates who are involved in church and community activities are going to get to know more potential patients. Professional association activity will be a plus, especially if the person is a subspecialist. A faculty position indicates that the person is current with new techniques and may enhance the practice image.

Management Experience: This is important for the future success of the practice. Look for knowledge in the business aspects of practice management; a plus would be marketing and management experience.

Everyone has a different agenda in terms of buyer selection. Whatever system you use to interview and select the right buyer, try to be consistent from candidate to candidate. Write down your reactions immediately after the interview. Otherwise, it is very easy to get confused after a few people have seen the practice. Usually it is very obvious who is the best candidate. If there is more than one suitable candidate, then further evaluation criteria will need to be used.

I find it very helpful to invite a serious candidate back to observe the practice for a few hours to see how patients are treated. This clinical exposure also will give you the opportunity to see how the person performs clinically, and how the person interacts with patients and staff. In addition, invite the finalist out to dinner with the spouses. A lot can be learned by listening to the spouse. Try to determine the level of commitment to the future practice transaction. Pay serious attention to the input offered by your own spouse.

Another excellent tool is to utilize your own staff. Try to set up a luncheon meeting with some of the important staff people and the candidate. Do not attend yourself, but be sure to find out the staff's reactions to the new person. Listen to what they say. In most cases, they can be excellent judges of character and probably can determine how well the new person will fit in with the practice and the patients. Getting the staff involved during this phase also will help to ease potential transition difficulties.

HOW SHOULD I HANDLE FINANCIAL INFORMATION?

It is up to you whether you want to disclose financial information at this time. If you are handling the sale yourself, and feel comfortable with the person, then it would be appropriate to give that person the appraisal of the practice. Discuss the various aspects of the appraisal but say no more about the practice price.

If a broker or consultant is handling the sale, leave all financial discussions in that person's hands. They know how to proceed from that point. This is one advantage to using an outside resource. It gets you out of the nego-tiating ballgame, and allows you to concentrate on the person and how that person will respond to the practice.

As the saying goes, "You can lead a horse to water, but you cannot make him drink." After numerous discussions with one client about the importance of not getting involved in the financial presentation of the practice, I discovered that the client gave up $30,000 to the buyer. How could this happen? Over lunch, the buyer and I negotiated an agreement that would result in the buyer paying full price for the practice plus the client's building. However, the buyer, being very sharp, went to see the client before I could make contact. When the seller and I talked to each other on the telephone later in the day, the client was very pleased that the buyer was going to buy the practice. The seller felt sorry for the buyer, knew his family, and offered the practice for $30,000 less than our agreement. Why? He felt (incorrectly) that the buyer could not afford to pay any more for the practice.

If you believe that you have found the proper buyer or buyers, then do some more background checking. Medical and dental licensing boards should be contacted, along with state and component societies. They can indicate the reputation of the person, any peer review complaints or licensing problems. For recent graduates, their medical or dental school faculty also should be contacted. If you know colleagues of the person, contact them for further reference checking. Also, get a financial statement from the person, and if possible a credit bureau report.

WHAT INFORMATION SHOULD I PROVIDE TO THE BUYER?

Serious buyers will need more information from you before they can proceed to the next stage, negotiating the terms of sale. The following information usually will be enough for the buyer's accountant and attorney to evaluate the practice:

- Practice appraisal
- Tax returns for the prior two to three years
- Financial statements for the prior two to three years
- List of accounts payable and liabilities
- Financial books and records of the practice
- Copies of any notes or mortgages owed that will not be paid off before the sale
- Existing contracts with health insurers, etc.
- Present lease

- Corporate books or partnership agreement, if any
- Sample patient charts
- List of aged accounts receivable, if they are to be included with the practice sale

HOW DO I NEGOTIATE EFFECTIVELY?

My experience indicates that the more aspects of the final practice sale that can be negotiated ahead of time, the better the results. An agreement at this stage will make it easier for the attorney to draw up the final contract of sale and will minimize the time required for the attorney.

The following tips, based on experience with actual practice sale situations, may be helpful during this process:

- Decide the price you want to sell the practice for and what the absolute minimum price will be. This results in an effective criterion to use during the negotiating process.

- If possible, handle all negotiations through a broker, accountant or attorney. Letters of agreement can be exchanged, and evaluated, better than during face-to-face negotiations. In addition, negative comments and distasteful events are shielded from you.

- If needed, when the practice sale is close to agreement, convene a meeting of the practice consultant, attorneys, and accountants for both sides. A fair and equitable agreement can be thrashed out during this meeting if problems have been encountered in the past.

- Do not use subterfuges, such as a hypothetical offer from someone else, to force the process. These gambits normally backfire. However, beware of the same strategy from the buyer's side, such as a low offer that is thrown onto the table only to test your resolve.

- Do not make any decisions that will force the sale of the practice to a particular buyer. For example, an agreement has been negotiated; but contracts have not been signed nor has money changed hands. Do not send out a letter of introduction to patients announcing the practice transfer. At closing the buyer can suddenly lower the offer, and you may be forced to sell at that lower price because steps already taken cannot be retracted. Contracts should be signed and money should have changed hands before implementing any practice changeover steps.

- Always look for creative ways to close the deal. As the attorney indicated at the beginning of the chapter, the terms of the sale are critical, not just the price.

Beware of the buyer who cannot make decisions himself or herself. Many a sale has been negated at the last minute because the buyer has brought in another person (such as the infamous brother-in-law), who can throw a monkey wrench into the final sale negotiations. Any outside person such as this, or a person who will be financing part of the sale, can bring up last-minute objections. Try to get everything on the table ahead of time and take care of objections at this stage.

HOW CAN NEGOTIATIONS GO WRONG?

Many potential practice sales are lost during this step because of negotiations getting out of hand. Both sides often start with extreme demands, hoping to compromise somewhere in the middle. Things go wrong when both parties get caught up in the struggle, and feel they have too much time, money and ego invested to adopt a conciliatory or problem-solving approach.

According to *Psychology Today* (June, 1986), there are at least four reasons why this breakdown in negotiations can occur. They are:

- Once you make an initial commitment to a position, you are more likely to notice information that supports the initial evaluation of the situation. This results in a closed mind.

- Your judgment is biased to interpret what you see and hear in a way that justifies your initial position.

- You want to save face, so you may increase your demands or hold out too long. This may happen even though it is against your best interests.

- Competitive nature may take over, adding to the likelihood of escalation. Reducing your demands may seem like defeat, while increasing them leaves the future uncertain. This seems more desirable than the certain loss of a concession, since you feel that the other side may be ready to cave in.

Recognizing these dangers is the first step to controlling them. The more knowledge about the situation that a person brings to the negotiating table, the more likely an equitable arrangement will be reached. Anticipate how the buyer is likely to be thinking and acting. Avoid pushing the buyer into a corner, getting him or her angry, or otherwise making the buyer feel that the struggle cannot be given up.

A major advantage of using a qualified practice consultant, broker or other professional is that the person should be an excellent third-party negotiator. A good adviser will strive to frame suggestions during an impasse in negotiations in ways that show what both sides will gain from a settlement. In one practice sale situation, the attorney led both parties through impasses in negotiations that I thought could never be breached. It was a delight to watch an expert in that situation bring an agreement out of almost guaranteed failure.

Negotiations actually begin at the time you first speak with a potential buyer. If you appear anxious to sell, the advantage tips to the buyer. Conversely, if the buyer appears anxious to purchase the practice, then you have the upper hand during negotiations. Listen to what the buyer is telling you through signals that are given during the process. If you listen well, are patient and consistent during the process, you will be successful.

Do not be greedy. One client received a very fair offer from a buyer. However, the client started adding last minute additions, such as wanting more money for supplies, a long-term employment contract that would guarantee the seller time in the practice after the sale, and new rent increases. The buyer recognized that the practice probably would fail from a financial standpoint if all of the new conditions were agreed to. The seller was trying to get as much out of the practice as possible, but probably would get nothing due to his greed. Luckily, the seller had a very astute attorney who was able to keep the practice negotiations on track, enable the seller to save face, and finalize a fair deal for both parties. This almost was lost because of the seller's attitude.

Another client met with a potential candidate and blurted out a practice price that was about 70% of what the final sale price should be. What possessed the seller to do this? He was afraid that his practice would not sell and did not want to lose this candidate. Luckily I was able to overcome this potentially serious financial mistake, but it was a close call.

The ultimate goal is to strike an agreement that is fair to both parties. A fair agreement will insure that the buyer can make the practice transfer successful. An unfair agreement, whether priced too high or with terms that will be impossible to meet, will result in disaster. Then both parties lose. A fair agreement results in a win-win situation.

WHAT ABOUT THE TAX CONSEQUENCES OF THE SALE?

How you treat the tax consequences of the practice sale depends upon your own philosophy. If you are conservative, then the majority of the sale probably will be taxed as ordinary income to you. If you are aggressive in postponing taxes, then most of the sale probably will be capital gains. It is imperative that good tax advice is utilized before signing the final contract of sale.

Personally, from a practice sale or normal investment standpoint, I always recommend structuring the deal first independent of the tax consequences. This conservative posture insures that any investment, or business situation, is examined first from a strictly economic standpoint. For example, if you are purchasing an apartment building, first determine if the building rents will carry the cash flow needs of the investment. If so, then the tax benefits will be a plus. If the building is in a negative cash flow situation, and tax benefits are necessary to see a positive return on investment, that may not be a sound investment choice.

The tax ramifications of a practice sale change almost yearly, depending upon which so-called Tax Reform Act

Congress has passed that year. The only certainty that I can guarantee is that given our government's insatiable appetite for spending, and its total lack of backbone concerning fiscal responsibility, taxes will continue to increase. Therefore, I cannot predict what the Tax Reform Act of 1999 will say about the tax deductibility of goodwill or its impact on capital gains, except that it will result in more taxes.

Generally, what will be a tax benefit for the seller will not be a benefit for the buyer, and vice versa. For example, what can be deducted as a depreciable asset by the buyer will be taxed as ordinary income for the seller. Once a practice sale has been structured and a price agreed upon, the final part needs to be negotiated—the tax consequences. The seller may be willing to give up some concessions in order to reduce his or her overall taxes from the sale. The buyer may be willing to increase the price somewhat, or shift part of the practice sale to a consulting agreement with the buyer, in order to deduct more of the practice sale as ordinary business expenses.

The following questions need to be answered by both the buyer and the seller in order to negotiate the final structure of the practice sale. These questions need to be answered by competent tax advisers, and then included in the final contract of sale.

Q: *What is the overall tax situation for each party?*

A: Normally, if the seller is approaching retirement, he or she will want to postpone income to later years, since overall income probably will be less after stopping practice. The buyer may want to postpone deductions, since he or she probably will not be in a higher tax bracket until after practicing for a few years.

Q: *Will the sale be treated as an installment sale, or will the entire amount of the sale be taxed immediately?*

A: Since most sales are structured as a long-term buy-out, if the entire amount of the sale price is taxable immediately, this can impact on the amount of cash down required by the seller. A higher cash down payment will be required in order to pay taxes.

Q: *What is the current status of capital gains taxation?*

A: If the capital gains rate is less than the ordinary income tax rate, then the seller will want to put more of the practice components into a capital gains situtation. Figure 16 describes the general treatment of capital gains in a practice sale.

    If capital gains taxation is less favorable to the seller than ordinary income, then some of the goodwill factors of the practice (covenant not to compete, for example) will need to be taken out of the total goodwill figure. For example, if the goodwill is estimated at $60,000, then $30,000 may need to be attributed to the covenant not to compete, $20,000 to a consulting fee payment over the life of the contract, $5,000 as patient chart value, and only $5,000 as the actual goodwill of the practice. Thus, all of these except for the $5,000 in goodwill will be taxed as ordinary income to the seller and deductible by the buyer.

Q: *If the practice is incorporated, will stock be sold to the buyer?*

A: If stock is sold, then the corporate tax rate may be more favorable to the seller. Or, deferred compensation may be utilized by the selling doctor. In any case, corporate stock generally is not sold, as the buyer may be picking up unknown future liabilities from past activities of the corporation.

Q: *Is the practice part of a partnership?*

A: Partnerships definitely require outside tax help. The complexities of each situation need to be addressed on a one-to-one basis.

Getting correct answers to these questions is critical—for both buyer and seller. The tax consequences of the sale may create some revisions in the final sale document. However, as stressed before, the overall agreement first

---

Figure 16

PRACTICE ASSETS VALUED:
TAX TREATMENT TO SELLER & BUYER

Asset	Seller	Buyer
Equipment & furnishings	Gain over basis	Depreciable
Leasehold improvements	Gain over basis	Depreciable
Buildings	Gain over basis (Part ordinary part capital)	Depreciable
Supplies	Ordinary income	Deductible
Accounts receivable	Ordinary income	N/A
Goodwill	Capital gain	Not deductible
Covenant not to compete	Ordinary income	Depreciable
Patient Charts	Status uncertain	Status uncertain
Consulting fee	Ordinary income	Deductible

should be constructed independent of the tax aspects in order to insure that the agreement is viable by itself. The tax tail never should wag the practice sale dog. Since the tax consequences can shift based upon the whims of politicians and bureaucrats, at least the quicksand will have a solid foundation under it.

WILL I GET THE APPRAISED VALUE FOR MY PRACTICE?

In my experience, most practices sell at the appraisal value unless outside circumstances preclude this. Such examples, from actual sales, include the following:

Disability: Practices which become available because the doctor has become disabled usually sell for less than the appraisal value. The selling doctor usually must sell quickly, the practice may have been deteriorating and the selling doctor is at a disadvantage during negotiations.

Death: Estate practice sales generally sell for much less than the appraised value of the practice if the doctor were still alive and active in the practice. It is vitally important the sale be consummated as soon as possible. Practice goodwill, meaning patient flow, drops dramatically and quickly after a doctor's death. The staff can be an important variable during this time. Positive reinforcement to patients will help keep the practice viable until a buyer can be located.

Financial Problems: If the practice has financial problems, or the doctor is declaring bankruptcy, then the sale price generally will drop. Banks, financial backers and buyers are hesitant to take over a practice with a questionable track record. Even if the changes necessary to improve the practice are easily recognized, buyers still will be hesitant. They are thinking—if the solution to the problem is this evident, why didn't the selling doctor make the changes already?

Time Restraints: A family practice physician had decided to move out of state and join a HMO. The doctor signed a contract obligating him to start in the new position within ninety days. This did not give enough time to find a buyer and dispose of his successful practice. Unfortunately, the practice was closed down, equipment wholesaled, and patients told to find other physicians. An OB/GYN wanted to sell her practice quickly, so the first buyer who appeared got a good deal because the selling doctor wanted to leave as soon as possible. A practice may sell within one month, or it may take years. On the average, at least six to twelve months should be planned for the practice sale process to be completed. Subspecialist practices may take even longer, due to the decreased number of potential buyers than for a general practice.

Without any of the above constraints, the sell price generally will be the appraised market value. In some instances, the sell price may be higher than the appraised value. For example, one doctor stayed on to assist the new doctor over a six-month period. He was paid a consultant's fee which was added to the practice price. Tax ramifications may enable the seller to get a higher price based upon tax consequences to the buyer.

Generally, you do not see the "dickering" that takes place in real estate sales. A house listed at $175,000 might be expected to sell for $165,000. This is based upon customary expectations in the real estate industry. So far, this concept has not impacted on practice sales.

WILL I GET CASHED OUT WHEN THE PRACTICE SELLS?

This is one of the most frequent questions that I get asked. Unfortunately, the answer is almost always "no." Very, very few practice sales are for cash. One problem is that there are not too many rich, young doctors out there. Actually, the phrase "a rich young doctor" is called an oxymoron. An oxymoron is a figure of speech in which contradictory terms are combined: for example, military intelligence— have you ever known the military to do anything intelligent? or jumbo shrimp—usually, the shrimp are so small that you need dissecting tweezers to eat them. The same is true for rich young doctors. Since a young doctor will be the most likely buyer, think about your own position in life after completing school. You probably were in debt, were just starting a family, and had no disposable income or assets. The same is true today, except more so. Therefore, very few practice sales are for cash.

Terms of sale generally are 20 to 30% cash down and the remainder paid off in three to seven years of monthly payments at a reasonable interest rate. In the normal sale, a bank or other financing concern usually will loan the purchaser enough for the down payment plus working capital. Working capital is needed for the buyer because the seller usually will keep the accounts receivable. Thus, the buyer will have to wait two to three months before collections will be at a normal rate, and will need to pay practice expenses and personal living expenses until this happens.

In many instances, the physical assets of the practice (equipment, furniture, instruments, and supplies) are used by the buyer as collateral for the loan. The remainder of the practice price is carried by the seller as a note to be repaid over a few years.

BUT WHAT ABOUT COLLATERAL?

If you read the above paragraph carefully you probably noticed that *your* practice assets were being utilized as collateral for *your* down payment. You may be thinking to yourself, "Ah, but this is very risky. If the practice fails, I will get it back, but the equipment will belong to the bank." This is true. In terms of collateral, an attorney is the best person to advise how this can be handled. Many buyers have homes or other assets which can be utilized to reduce the risk and exposure of the practice. Others may have relatives who are willing to co-sign the note or put up collateral for the practice. However, in many cases it is impossible to collateralize totally the practice sale. The financing institution generally will file a lien on the equipment collateral. You can file a secondary position lien, but it is more of a psychological benefit than anything else. By the time the equipment may be sold to satisfy the first lien there usually is not too much left over for other creditors. As indicated previously in this book, many times the bottom line is a judgment call of the buyer's character and ability to keep the practice successful.

HOW IS THE REMAINDER OF THE PRICE PAID?

The remainder of the practice price is carried as a note from the buyer to the seller. Usual terms are three to seven years for the pay-out, at a fixed interest rate that reflects current conditions. The prime rate (or prime rate plus one or two percentage points) is used many times. Usually the interest rate is set at a level that is more than you could obtain by investing the money in treasury notes or money market funds, and less than the buyer would have to pay for bank financing. Banks generally will not loan the entire amount of the purchase price. In the "good old days" doctors could get signature loans for about any amount that they wanted. Reality today is that most loans must be collateralized.

Many contracts include the interest rate as a variable. That is, the interest rate is redetermined every year, based on changes in the banking prime rate or the rate of inflation. Upper and lower limits sometimes are added to preclude wide fluctuations from year to year that can upset financial planning by the buyer or seller.

The interest rate also may be affected by the amount of collateral, if any, available to secure the practice loan. With more collateral, and theoretically less risk, the interest rate might be negotiated lower.

WHERE DOES THE BUYER FIND THE DOWN PAYMENT FINANCING?

The seller's bank usually is the best place for the new buyer to start. Your bank probably has known you and the practice for a number of years. They will not want to lose your account, and thus will try to help the buyer. Personally introduce the buyer to the banker. Doing this will also give you an excellent idea as to the credit worthiness of the buyer. Banks will do a very thorough credit check. Thus, if they approve the buyer for a loan, you usually can be assured that the buyer is a good credit risk. This will increase the probability of the note being paid off. You can check out the buyer's credit rating yourself or have an attorney or CPA do it. However, your local banker probably is the best person to do this.

WHAT ABOUT THE TERMS OF THE PRACTICE SALE NOTE?

The terms of the pay-out for your share of the practice note are usually three to seven years. The average is five years. This is a reasonable time frame for the buyer. After five years, the equipment and reception room furniture may need replacing, so the money that was used for the pay-out could be used then for equipment and furniture purchases. A level monthly pay-out, with interest and principal repayment, is the best path to follow. In some instances, sellers will take interest only during the first six months, as a way of easing the buyer into a favorable financial position. This is up to you, but a financially healthy practice should not need this concession. Also, beware of balloon payments, such as having the buyer only pay interest for the first two to three years, then the entire balance of the note at once. The discipline of making monthly interest and principal payments is better than postponing principal payments.

WHAT IF I ALSO HAVE A FACILITY TO SELL?

About 60% of practice sales also involve a facility. Naturally, most sellers want to sell their building at the same time, especially if it is a single use, single office building. However, the buyer may be scared to take on additional debt for the building. Many times a right of first refusal is built into the sale contract. This gives the buyer the right to match any reasonable offer that you may receive for the building in the future. In other cases, a building price is agreed upon at the time of sale of the practice, and the building is sold at a later date to the buyer for this price. Or, appraisals could be done later and the price fixed based upon these appraisals. After a few years, most buyers realize that they are better off building equity in their building rather than just paying rent. When the buyer comes to this realization, then the building usually can be sold quickly.

Your individual tax situation may make it advantageous for you to postpone the sale of the building until later. Individual situations vary considerably. In one instance, the facility became the vehicle for obtaining the cash down payment for the practice. Many banks prefer to loan on real estate. Thus, the building was refinanced by the buyer, part of the building down payment was used for the practice down payment, and the seller was able to secure a second mortgage on the building as collateral for the practice sale.

If you are not selling the facility, make sure that a reasonable rent is charged to the buyer. You already may have paid off the building, and only need to make property tax, insurance and maintenance expense pay-outs. Basing the rent on these expenses may understate the true rent that should be charged.

WHAT IS THE NEXT STEP?

When the basics of the practice sale have been negotiated, such as price, down payment, interest rate, payback period, timing and changeover plan, it is time to have an earnest money agreement completed. This agreement will outline the basics of the sale negotiations, commit the buyer to purchasing the practice, and commit you to take the practice off the market. Usually, $500 to $2,000 is adequate for an earnest money payment by the potential buyer. Once this is signed, the buyer can back out of the practice sale only if down payment financing cannot be arranged.

HOW DO I DRAW UP AN EARNEST MONEY AGREEMENT?

A standard real estate earnest money agreement or a business sale agreement can be utilized. Separate agreements need to be drawn up for the practice and the facility, if any. Your attorney can assist in this if desired. Most practice brokers and consultants also provide generic earnest money arrangements. The money can be deposited by the attorney into a trust account. If the buyer backs out after this, except for not being able to obtain financing, then the earnest money is yours.

I have never had a practice sale not be completed because financing could not be arranged. It may take some creative efforts on everyone's part, but this should not be a deterrent to the eventual sale of the practice.

The usual term for the earnest money agreement is thirty to sixty days. This gives the buyer enough time to arrange financing and gives you time to have a contract of sale drawn up. Do not let the term go beyond this, since the practice should not be taken off the market for an indefinite time period. It may preclude a sale to someone else.

The importance of the earnest money was brought home recently with an experience that taught me a lesson in practice sales. A buyer had been considering the purchase of an out-of-state practice, had several telephone discussions with me and the selling doctor, investigated schools and the community, and was planning on bringing his family to see the practice and the community. One week before this trip was scheduled, another buyer was found. This new buyer purchased the practice and the doctor's building in one weekend, thus leaving the original candidate out in the cold. It was very discouraging to call this doctor on the following Monday and tell him to cancel his trip and plans. Understandably, he was very upset. The moral for buyers—it is better to check out the practice personally, and then get the family involved if the practice looks feasible. An earnest money agreement in this case would have saved considerable grief for the buyer.

In some instances it will be proper to have a longer term earnest money agreement. For example, two practices recently were sold to doctors graduating about eight months in the future. The earnest money agreements will save the practices for these doctors.

Once the earnest money agreement is accepted by the seller, then the practice is about 90% sold.

8

LEGAL AND FINANCIAL CONSIDERATIONS

"The ultimate purpose of any
contract, one which lawyers can't
understand, is not to get a
stranglehold on the other party, but
to formalize an understanding that is
of real and proportionate benefit to
both sides over time."*

Once the earnest money agreement has been completed, the practice sale process moves into the legal arena. The contract of sale needs to be drawn up at this time. It is the basis for solving any future misunderstanding or problems with the practice sale. Therefore, expert legal help is essential.

Lawyers and doctors never have been good bedfellows. The cyclical crises in malpractice insurance always seem to end up with finger pointing by both sides. One way to understand the malpractice situation is to look at statistics. We all know that the population:doctor ratio has been

---

decreasing for both physicians and dentists. What is also interesting is the fact that the ratio of population:lawyers is even worse. The ratio is about 360:1. Thus, for every physician there is at least one attorney; and for every dentist there are about four attorneys. The scramble for clients by attorneys is even more demanding than the search for patients by doctors.

However, in this instance expert legal advice is a requirement for the successful sale of the practice. The key to success in dealing with attorneys, though, is to keep in mind that attorneys are there to implement *your* needs, not theirs. Do not let the mumbo-jumbo of legalese disrupt your need to design a contract of sale that is fair for both parties concerned. The success of the practice sale, and thus the financial pay-out for the sale will depend upon the success of the new buyer. Hurdles designed to trip up this success will backfire, with the loser being the seller.

This reminds me of a story that I heard. The word "solicitor," in England, means attorney. The same word, solicitor, in France, means prostitute. Some people believe that you end up with the same results from both of them. However, this does not have to be the case if certain criteria are followed.

Utilize an attorney who has experience with health care practice sales. Just as doctors may be subspecialists, so are attorneys. A divorce lawyer may not be the best attorney to use for a contract sale. Use an attorney who has references in this field. Check out those references before proceeding. Selling a practice can be a risky and expensive process, so make sure the sale contract is the best that can be obtained.

It is also important that the buyer retain an attorney to review the contract of sale and other legal documents. In this way both parties are protected. In the majority of cases, the seller is responsible for the contract of sale. It makes good sense to take charge of this aspect of the practice sale, since you want to protect your assets and practice in the future.

WHAT ABOUT USING SAMPLE CONTRACTS?

As a shortcut, some doctors utilize the sample sale contracts available from medical and dental associations. Others copy contracts that colleagues have used. If you do this to save money, the results may be very expensive. These contracts are only outlines. Utilize them only as a reference for your own custom contract. Every practice sale is unique, so a custom-designed contract makes a lot of sense. Utilize sample contracts only as a reference for your own custom contract.

WHAT OTHER LEGAL DOCUMENTS MAY BE REQUIRED?

In addition to the practice sale contract, other documents may have to be drawn up. These include the following:

Lease: If you own the facility, and it is not being sold with the practice at this time, then a lease agreement needs to be completed.

Employment Agreement: If you are coming back into the practice as a part-time associate or employee, agreements need to be completed.

Guarantees: If someone other than the buyer also is helping to finance or collateralize the sale, then these guarantees may need to be done separately from the contract of sale.

Facility Contract of Sale: Selling the facility will also require a separate legal document.

There may be other documents that are required depending upon your needs.

All of these documents should be completed, given to the buyer, and revisions made if necessary. They should all be signed at the practice closing. Try not to leave any loose ends for later completion. The results may not be to your liking, as the following case history illustrates:

> A practice was sold, unfortunately as part of an estate, because of the sudden death of the doctor. A letter of agreement was signed, but final practice sale contracts were not. After being in the practice for a couple of months, the buyer decided that he did not like the practice and refused to complete the sale. The estate was left with a worthless practice, except for some equipment.

This could have been avoided easily if the necessary contracts had been signed before the practice changed hands.

WHAT SHOULD BE INCLUDED IN THE CONTRACT OF SALE?

The following areas, at a minimum, should be addressed in the contract:

Terms of sale, including the sale price, down payment and financing. The earnest money agreement is the basis for this.

Default conditions and a mechanism for taking back the practice in case of buyer default. This certainly is not expected, but all contingencies need to be covered.

The seller's obligations during the changeover, such as the amount of time to be spent helping the buyer, remuneration for the seller's production time in the practice, letter of introduction to the patients, accounts receivable disposition, and any rework clauses.

Collateral for the practice note.

Insurance requirements, such as life insurance on the buyer to be paid to the seller, disability insurance on the buyer, fire and commercial insurance on the property, and practice and malpractice insurance.

A non-compete clause so that the buyer will be protected from the seller opening up another practice in the same general area. It is surprising how many doctors may change their minds about their future plans. This is not a problem with retirement, but changes in careers and relocation sometimes do not work out. In these cases the buyer needs to be protected. Restrictions should not be so harsh that a court might not enforce them. Restrictive clauses must be reasonable as to the nature of the limitation, the time constraint, and the geographic distance involved (*Dental Management,* August, 1985).

Access to patient records by the seller. The seller needs to be able to consult past records in case of later malpractice problems.

Telephone and practice name utilization by the buyer. Most contracts of sale also include both buyer's and seller's warranties. These are items that buyer and seller state as virtual fact and are willing to back up with very strong assurances. It is important to understand this part of the sales contract. In Appendix B, sample warranty language is shown with examples of what the warranties mean. This is provided as an example, and should not be used without the advice of counsel. The information is from an article by Randall K. Berning, J.D., in *Dentistry Today* (August, 1987).

Besides drawing up the contract of sale, the attorney may be able to conclude negotiations on aspects of the practice sale that have not been completed. A good third-party facilitator is a dream to watch in action. Coming to a final agreement is like watching a ballet—choreographed by the attorney. On the other hand, when attorneys for both sides get into an adversarial situation, the picture is not so pretty.

One client commented, after spending one and one-half hours concluding a practice sale agreement with the buyer, attorneys for both sides and myself, that this was one of the worst meetings of his life. The attorneys were arguing over aspects of the sale that had been concluded much earlier. As the doctor commented, he purchased his first practice thirty years ago over lunch with the seller. The contract was on the back of a napkin. How times do change!

WHAT ROLE SHOULD INSURANCE PLAY IN THE CONTRACT?

One excellent way to reduce the risk involved with selling (or buying) a practice is the protection offered by insurance. You may be thinking only about the role that life insurance plays in your own estate planning, but with the products offered today, practice risks can be reduced significantly also. This protection is for the benefit of both the buyer and seller.

Insurance products to consider, and their role in the sale include:

Life insurance: The seller needs to be protected in case of the death of the buyer for the duration of the sale contract. By purchasing decreasing term insurance, the buyer can obtain inexpensive insurance protection. The beneficiary of the policy should be the seller or the seller's estate. Thus, if the buyer should die before the contract is paid off, the insurance proceeds will pay off the seller, and the buyer's estate can dispose of the practice without having the contract of sale liability.

In some instances, the buyer may want to purchase an insurance policy on the life of the seller. Since the seller is usally older, the cost of this coverage may be prohibitive, but in the event of the death of the seller, the insurance proceeds would pay off the balance of the contract.

Practice Overhead Insurance: Since a younger buyer is eight times as likely to become disabled for ninety days or more than to die, this protection makes a lot of sense. Overhead insurance will pay the expenses of the practice while the buyer is disabled. The insurance may not pay principal payments to the seller for the practice note, but it should pay interest. In addition, it will insure that the practice stays viable while a locum tenens is running the practice. It also is possible to obtain an insurance policy that will pay the locum tenens' salary as well.

Disability Insurance: Personal disability insurance will pay the buyer while he or she is disabled. In addition, a portion of the monthly payment can be assigned to pay the seller the principal part of the practice note.

When purchasing disability insurance, it is important to choose the correct waiting period. Many policies are sold with a ninety-day wait. This means that the policy will not pay until the insured has been disabled for at least one hundred and twenty days. However, by this time accounts receivable are depleted, and there is a chance that the practice may go bankrupt. The recommended waiting period is thirty days. This then would provide a payment from the insurance policy on the sixtieth day.

Malpractice Insurance: Obviously, this is a require-ment for any doctor. Without it, the seller runs the risk that the assets of the practice will be sold or attached to satisfy any claims; in addition, the buyer may be forced into bankruptcy.

Commercial Coverage: This coverage is to protect the buyer from losses caused by perils, such as fire, and claims arising from patient injuries, such as falling on stairs.

The cost for these coverages is minimal when the benefits to both seller and buyer are calculated.

WHAT OCCURS DURING THE PRACTICE CLOSING MEETING?

Once all of the contracts and financing arrangements have been completed, it is time for closing. This generally is a meeting of the buyer, seller, attorneys, and possibly accountants and practice consultants. By the time of closing, everything should have been completed. Some final tasks that take place are the following:

- Bulk sale contract notices, if required, need to be sent to suppliers and creditors
- Cashier checks are needed for the down payment and any closing costs such as taxes, commissions or other bills
- Insurance binders
- Employee benefits changeovers

The closing usually is a very good meeting. All of the negotiations should have been completed already, so no surprises are expected. Everyone is optimistic about the future, and a spirit of cooperation should be evident.

The closing must be in the hands of your attorney. Proceed with his or her direction and the sale will be concluded successfully.

Congratulations! The practice has been sold. However, before the champagne is broken out, a very important element of the practice sale process needs to be initiated. This is the transition from the seller being in charge of the practice and the patients to the buyer assuming these functions. The next chapter will consider this critical phase.

Another situation to be alert to after the contract has been signed, but before the practice changeover occurs, is "buyer remorse." This also is known by psychologists as "cognitive dissonance." The best example is when a new car has been purchased. After buying the car the owner suddenly will notice how many cars of the same make are on the road. The buyer's senses are alert to this. Even magazine, newspaper and radio advertisements for this brand are read in detail, after the purchase. Many car manufacturers actually design ads for this after-sale situation. The buyer is looking for reinforcement concerning the purchase decision.

Anxious reconsideration sometimes can undo a deal that already has been consummated. I make it a point to call the buyer a few days after the closing meeting. The purpose of the call is to reinforce the positive reasons for purchasing the practice. Sellers often have the same problem. Therefore, the seller also is contacted to make sure that "seller's remorse" does not rear its ugly head. This process is normal with every sale situation. Facing the situation will insure that the practice transition phase will proceed smoothly.

9

THE SUCCESSFUL TRANSITION

HOW MANY PATIENTS WILL THE PRACTICE LOSE?

A buyer wants a practice because of the likelihood that patients will stay with the practice, and this gives the buyer a head start on the future. The transition stage is critical in order to maintain this patient flow. Expect some patient drop-off. The most common reason is commuting distance. Patients who live a long way from the practice may choose a doctor closer to their home, since they may have been traveling the longer distance only because of the seller.

Horror stories abound concerning the loss of patients when a practice is sold. One internal medicine resident was not interested in a very successful practice in a major city because he had heard that you normally lose about 50% of the patients when a practice changes hands. The sources of such misinformation are difficult to find, since my experience does not indicate that a severe patient drop-off will occur if certain basic principles are followed during the changeover.

A buyer should not expect more than a 10% to 15% loss of patients. Usually, after one year, the practice is at or above the level it was before the purchase. The buyer will bring in his or her own circle of contacts, who replace former patients lost to the practice. In many instances, the practice will be 10 to 20% above its former level. The energy, and sometimes extra hours, put in by the buyer pays off in terms of new patient growth.

The key principle to follow during the initial changeover is to *not make any changes*. Changes in a practice routine, staff, location or layout can be upsetting to patients. The patient should see as little change as possible, except for the treating doctor. Since changes can be stressful, they need to be minimized.

HOW LONG SHOULD THE TRANSITION PERIOD BE?

In most practice changeovers, the seller will remain for thirty to sixty days to assist in the changeover. Ideally, if it is possible to bring the buyer in one to two years ahead of time, the best possible result can be had. This way the patients get used to the new person before the seller leaves the practice. Another good strategy is to have the seller continue practicing on a reduced basis for a few months or years. Patients who insist on seeing the former doctor can be worked into that doctor's schedule, but since scheduled appointments may not be available immediately, the staff has a natural opening to ease the patient into the new doctor's schedule.

In many instances, gradual transition periods have worked very well. One client came back to his practice as an associate for one and one-half days for the first six months after the practice sale, one day per week for the next six months, and one-half day per week for the next six months. After eighteen months the seller finally retired full time to his "second career." Another client has been seeing patients one day per week for the past three years. In yet another instance, the buyer is assuming 25% of the practice each year for four years. After four years the transition will be complete.

As a seller, you need to be prepared to stop practicing completely. If the practice cannot justify another doctor financially, or personality clashes cause the relationship between buyer and seller to disintegrate, the seller must step aside. If not, the future success of the entire transaction may be in jeopardy. As a buyer, the best route to follow is to predicate any agreement concerning future involvement of the seller in the practice on the financial results of the practice transfer.

Many clients expect to spend six months or longer in the normal transition. Where it is not possible for the transition period to be a few years, it is usually better to get it over with as soon as possible. Therefore, I recommend a thirty- to sixty-day period for a normal transition. Why so short a period? Usually, after thirty days the "honeymoon" period of the practice transition is starting to wear thin. The buyer wants to assume total control of the practice, which will not happen as long as the seller still is involved. The seller may object to some of the differences in routine introduced by the buyer; sometimes the seller has sabotaged the practice transfer because of this. I guess the adage that too many cooks spoil the broth applies in this case.

Now may be the time to put together an office policy manual, if one is not already available. The office manual should contain employee job descriptions, front office procedures, clinical procedures, office policies, employee benefit programs, and patient and surgery scheduling criteria. This manual can act as a foundation for the management aspects of the practice transfer.

HOW SHOULD PATIENTS AND REFERRING DOCTORS BE INTRODUCED?

It is not necessary for the seller to introduce personally every patient to the buyer. The staff, and other transitional activities, will take care of this function. The seller wants to introduce the buyer to the office routines and procedures, community contacts, hospital personnel, and colleagues. However, if the practice is a subspecialty with other referring doctors, it is critical that time be spent introducing the buyer to *every* member of the referral network. Now is the time to collect for all those favors the referring doctors may owe you. The future success of your practice sale depends on keeping those referring doctors in the practice.

HOW WILL STAFF LOYALTY BE TRANSFERRED?

Longevity of staffing, expecially in the reception area, is a plus for the goodwill of the practice. If the staff will stay, at least during the changeover, it will improve patient retention. Patients probably know the staff better than the doctor, and if the receptionist and others are very positive with patients concerning the transfer of the practice, the patients are much more likely to stay.

As an example of this, a doctor recently died of a heart attack. It took about six weeks to appraise the practice, find a buyer, and complete the contract of sale. During this time the receptionist single-handedly kept the practice together. Her positive spirit and attitude resulted in the loss of only two patients during this critical time period.

Tell the staff that the buyer is now the boss. You appreciate and value the contributions that the staff has made in the past and know that they will continue to do so in the future. People being the way they are, staff loyalty usually transfers completely the first time the buyer signs the payroll checks!

With dentists, the hygienist also plays an important role during the transition. During the prophylaxis the patient can be prepared for the changeover to a new dentist if the hygienist uses a positive attitude with the patient. For physicians with a physician's assistant, the assistant also can ease the transition of patient loyalty to the new physician.

WHAT ABOUT A LETTER OF INTRODUCTION?

A well-written letter of introduction to patients will enhance the retention rate. Indicate why you are leaving, your appreciation for their loyalty, your enthusiasm about the buyer, his or her background and practice philosophy, staff retention, and your confidence in the future. The buyer also may want to enclose a letter describing his or her excitement about assuming the practice and philosophy of practice.

I always recommend that a photograph be enclosed if possible. It does not cost much to include a photograph with the letter of introduction. In this way the patients can see the buyer and seller together, and associate a face with the buyer. The letter should be sent out within the first ninety days of the transfer. Sometimes it is a good idea to delay the letter until the buyer has been with the practice for a few weeks. This way both you and the buyer will be more comfortable discussing the changeover with the patients. This is an excellent time to try to reactivate patients who have not been in the practice for awhile.

If you have a practice newsletter, include information about the transfer in the newsletter, along with pictures if possible.

The wording of the letter needs to reflect your thoughts and personality. The following letter (Figure 17) is from an actual practice sale. It is one of the best that I have ever seen. It really gets the patient involved in the doctor's decision to retire, superbly introduces the new doctor, and encourages the patient to continue with the practice. Obviously not everyone could write such a letter sincerely. However, it demonstrates that the selling doctor's personality is an important element of the letter of introduction.

HOW LONG SHOULD MY NAME BE LEFT ON THE DOOR?

The period of time that the selling doctor's name is associated with the practice will depend upon many variables. If the doctor is coming back as an associate, then the name can be a part of the practice for as long as the doctor remains. If the doctor is leaving, then the length of time may vary depending upon the individual state practice act. Usually, one year is the most common time frame. The telephone book listing also should be continued for as long as possible. The telephone should be answered by the receptionist using both doctors' names during this period.

Figure 17

LETTER OF INTRODUCTION

Dear Friends,

Please consider this a personal letter, even though it is being sent to many, many people.

I have good news and good news. Many of you are aware that in addition to being unable so far to arrest my own aging process, my wife's health is such that I could conceivably be forced to stop practice almost without notice. This is not the way I want to treat you who have become faithful patients and friends. The good news is, I have found a highly qualified doctor, whom I trust to take care of my "family" of patients, who is willing to take over my practice. More good news: he has invited me and our entire staff to stay and work with him until I have to step down or until all of you decide it's time to move over to a younger (better looking?) doctor.

My choice for my replacement is Dr. Younger, who has been practicing in Honolulu, Hawaii, but who is really a native of our state. He is thirty-four years old, exactly the age I was when I came to this city. His beautiful wife is a physical therapist at the hospital. Dr. Younger has lived here before, when he was a medical x-ray technician at the hospital. He is a graduate of _____, recognized as one of the finest schools in the country.

I am happy and excited over this important change, and more aware than usual of how much your support and friendship have meant to my wife and myself. Now I have one favor to ask: I will feel honored if you will continue the confidence you have shown in me by whole-heartedly accepting my "replacement." I feel sure you will be pleased with his gentle manner and dedication to excellence.

Very Sincerely,

Dr. Wiser

SHOULD THE FEE SCHEDULE BE CHANGED?

It is important that the buyer not make any changes in the fee schedule during the first six months of the transfer. Ideally, the fees have been kept current and at prevailing rates for the community. Patients will react negatively to a new doctor who immediately increases fees. If the fee schedule is below average, try to change it before the practice transfer occurs. If this is not possible, try to get the buyer to increase it on a gradual basis, rather than make a big jump immediately.

WHAT ABOUT PRACTICE MARKETING?

The transition stage is an excellent practice marketing opportunity. The letter of introduction will reactivate many inactive patients. In addition, go through all of your old charts, separating them into two piles—the first pile for those patients who are no longer a part of the practice; the second, those who need encouragement to come back to the practice or who need medical or dental attention. Besides getting a letter of introduction, these patients should be contacted by telephone or personal letter and told of their potential need to see a doctor.

This also is a good time to have an open house. It enables you to say goodby to your patients and for them to meet the new doctor in a less stressful situation. The following open house invitation (Figure 18) was sent out by one of my clients. The results were excellent.

As a result of the open house, many formerly inactive patients came, met the buyer, Dr. Eager, and are now active patients. You might suggest that the buyer send out a questionnaire asking patients for comments and suggestions about improving the practice. Focus on patient needs and do not let the survey become a critique of your practice. Patients appreciate being asked their opinions and will feel that the buyer is asking them to stay with the practice.

Figure 18
OPEN HOUSE INVITATION

Dear Patient:

Dr. Pleasant is proud to announce the transfer of his practice to Dr. Eager, and would like to invite you to attend an OPEN HOUSE on Sunday, November 15, in his office.

Please join us for this opportunity to get to know Dr. Eager and visit our office. There will be free informational brochures available, and Dr. Eager will be happy to answer any of your health-related questions.

Hours will be from 11:00 a.m. to 5:00 p.m., and refreshments will be served.

If you are unable to attend, please feel free to drop by anytime, or call us.

Sincerely,

Dr. Pleasant   Dr. Eager

WHAT ABOUT NEWSPAPER PUBLICITY?

Contact the local newspaper and try to get some free publicity with a news story concerning the practice changeover. See if you can come up with an interesting angle or subject for the article. Perhaps you are planning on embarking on a new career that will interest readers, or the buyer has some interesting special skills or hobbies. This is a valuable marketing tool for reaching established and potential new patients.

The following article was found in *The Vail Trail*, the newspaper for the ski resort town of Vail, Colorado (October 2, 1987):

New Doctor Joins Clinic

Dr. Downhill has joined the Vail Mountain Medical Clinic. His specialty is internal medicine.

Downhill is a graduate of _____ University and has a medical degree from _____ University. Before moving to Vail, he completed his residency training in internal medicine at _____.

Downhill said during the end of his residency, he noticed an ad in a medical journal about the position in Vail. Downhill, his wife and five-month-old daughter came to Vail for a visit and interview. Both went well.

"We loved the mountains and skiing," Downhill said. "This is a rare place. It's a small community but is cosmopolitan and can support a specialist."

Downhill said his specialty deals with the medical problems of adolescents and adults. The problems include those concerning the heart, lungs, metabolism, infections, arthritis, digestion, and the blood.

He also performs exercise testing for cardiac evaluation, and emphasizes preventive medicine. Downhill said the most common health problem he sees in his practice is adult high blood pressure.

The doctor also focuses his practice on hospital medicine. Downhill said he enjoys his work. "I went into medicine because I felt like I could help people," he said. "I can't always cure them, but I can make them feel better."

Originally from _____, in his free time he plans to ski and he enjoys other outdoor activities including Nordic skiing, mountain biking, and backpacking. Downhill and his wife are avid readers and enjoy the arts.

"We are excited to be in Vail and are looking forward to becoming part of this community," he said.

Downhill is at the clinic each weekday and can be reached by calling. . . ."

ARE THERE ANY FINAL THOUGHTS TO CONSIDER?

As a final thought, watch out for the negative role that criticism can play in the transition. Emphasize to the buyer that patients will be wary at first and may be looking for reasons to stop coming to the practice. Therefore, it is important that all patients are treated with respect and not in a hurried manner. Actually, this makes good sense at any time, but especially during the changeover. Try to get across to the buyer that he or she may practice in a different style, but that patients should not be told that their former treatment was incorrect or inferior.

Everyone has made mistakes in the past. Now is not the time to dwell on them with patients. For example, in the personnel area, whenever a new staff member is added, you almost can guarantee that the new person will find fault with the former employee in that position. This is called the "new employee syndrome." The same thing may happen to you. However, patients will be hypersensitive to any critical or disparaging comments made by the buyer about the seller. This sensitivity can result in patient loss if the patient perceives that the buyer is criticizing the previous standard of care.

Conversely, watch yourself when discussing treatment plans with the buyer or with patients. Do not criticize the buyer in front of patients or staff.

WHEN WILL THE MOST SUCCESSFUL TRANSITION OCCUR?

Most transitions are successful. In my experience, the most successful transitions occur when there is a high degree of trust and respect between the selling doctor and the patients. By communicating your faith and enthusiasm for the person taking over the practice, you will find the patients will keep on trusting your judgment by transferring their care to the new person. That is the basis for a successful transition.

WHAT ABOUT THE FUTURE?

Most of my clients find that instead of retirement, they are embarking on a new career. Remember, age does not limit productivity. One of my clients is enjoying his career as a cruise ship doctor; another is a commercial real estate agent; a third is an insurance salesperson; a fourth is a dental school professor; and one is on a leisurely trip around the world. Many options are available.

I have never had an unsuccessful practice sale. If you follow the principles discussed in this book, I am sure that you, too, will have a successful practice transfer. As Ben Franklin said in *The Way to Wealth*—

DILIGENCE IS THE MOTHER
OF GOOD LUCK.

SAMPLE PRACTICE APPRAISAL

January 15, 1988

TO: Clark Kent, M.D.
FROM: Gary Schaub
SUBJECT: Clinic Appraisal

The following represents an appraisal of the value of your medical clinic. The appraisal is based upon information supplied by you, your staff and your CPA; it includes a complete inspection of the assets of the clinic, investigation of background material, and analysis of the clinic.

I. OBJECTIVE

The objective of this report is to estimate the market value of the clinic. The approach used to determine market value was based on the market value valuation technique. Comparisons to similar clinics that have been sold recently plus an analysis and evaluation of the practice factors that influence the final market value estimate were also utilized.

I certify that I have personally inspected the clinic and that employment for this appraisal is not in any manner contingent on returning appraisal findings in any specified or implied amount or otherwise contingent on anything else other than the delivery of this report. To the best of my knowledge and belief, all the statements and opinions contained in this report are correct. This appraisal has been made in conformity with the professional ethics and standards of professional conduct of national appraisal organizations.

II. QUALIFYING AND LIMITING CONDITIONS

The information identified in this report as being furnished by others is believed to be reliable, but no responsibility for accuracy is assumed.

Possession of this report, or a copy, does not carry with it the right of publication, nor may it be used for any purpose by anyone but the client without the consent of the appraiser.

The appraiser's background includes eight years of dental and medical practice management consulting and the appraisal and/or sale of over $25,000,000 worth of practices. Educational background includes a Bachelor of Science in Electrical Engineering and a Masters in Business Administration. The appraiser is a Clinical Instructor in Practice Management at the Oregon Health Sciences University. Professional and client references are available on request.

III. FACILITY

A. Background

The office is located at 101 Medical Center Plaza, Metropolis, Kansas. The building was built about 1967. A chiropractor and an optometrist are located in the facility. The office contains about 2,500 sq. ft. It has a reception area, reception office, private office, business office, five exam rooms, lab, lounge, and an x-ray area.

B. Parking

Off-street parking is provided.

C. Location

The office is located close to the downtown area of Metropolis. It is on a major north/south arterial with a high traffic flow and is easy to locate. The surrounding area contains professional offices, residences, retail stores, apartments, and schools. The demographics of the area are excellent, as there is a large shopping center, fast-food outlets, and other traffic-dependent services in the immediate area. Metropolis has a population of 94,000, and the metropolitan area has a population of 258,000. The twenty-four hour traffic count for the nearest intersection, Dorothy Street— Constance Avenue, is as follows:

1981	1982	1983	1984	1985
22,160	21,800	19,580	23,100	24,400

This is the fifth highest count in Metropolis.

The Population Age Distribution is as follows:

18-24 years	13.7%
25-34	20.7%
35-49	16.8%
50 +	26.3%

The Median Household Effective Buying Income is as follows:

$10,000 - 19,999	30.6%
$20,000 - 34,999	27.4%
$35,000 - 49,999	6.4%

D. Rent

The rent is $1,900 per month. The lease expires in 1992, with a five-year extension.

The landlord has indicated that the present lease can be extended for five years beyond its present 1997 expiration.

E. Appearance

The building and grounds are well-maintained. The reception area and operatories present a somewhat cluttered initial impression.

F. Ownership

The building is not owned by Dr. Kent. However, the owner has indicated that the sale of the property to the new clinic owner is a possibility, if desired.

APPRAISED VALUE   *Not Appraised*

IV. PATIENT RECORDS

There are about 3,000 to 3,500 active patients in the practice for the past two years.

V. GOODWILL

A. Practice Age

Dr. Kent has been in practice for twenty years, and at this location for seven years.

B. Type of Practice

The practice is general family practice. No OB is done. Minor surgery is done in the office, with fractures and D & Cs done in the hospital. The call is handled by the Emergency Room at Metropolis Memorial Hospital. Dr. Kent is a Board-Certified Family Practice physician and is on the staff of the hospital.

The charge breakdown for the month of October, 1987, is as follows: Lab–6%; X-Ray–12%; Patient Charges–81%.

C. Location

Good location in Metropolis, Kansas.

D. Staff

Receptionist/Insurance Clerk—Works five days per week. Has been with the practice for two years.

Medical Assistant (2)— They have been with practice for an average of two years. They are cross-trained in all positions and have x-ray licenses.

E. Patient Load and Demographics

The clinic is open 9:00 a.m.–6:00 p.m. Monday through Thursday, and Friday, 9:00–12:00. Dr. Kent works four and one-half days per week. He sees about two hundred patients per week.

The patients come from blue collar and middle class backgrounds. Very few welfare patients are seen. About twenty-five percent are age eighteen or younger and about five percent are over age sixty-five.

Cash is preferred for billings under forty dollars. About fifty percent of the patients pay cash; the rest is insurance.

F. Fee Schedule

The fees are at or above prevailing rates for a family practice clinic. They were last updated in the fall of 1986.

G. Practice Promotion

Very little marketing is done. A clinic brochure is given to patients and there is a Yellow Page advertisement. Dr. Kent gives talks to community groups.

Dr. Kent is a member of the American Medical Association, Kansas Medical Association, and the County Component Society. He graduated from the University and had one year of surgery residency.

H. New Doctor Introduction

Dr. Kent will assist in the changeover of the practice and will send an announcement letter to all active patients.

I. Non-Compete Covenant

Dr. Kent will sign a reasonable non-compete covenant for private practice medicine. He does not want to continue working in the practice.

J. Financial

	1985	1986	1987
Collections	$312,288	$327,720	$341,015
Expenses	171,756	160,582	173,917
Net Income	140,532	167,138	167,098
Net Income	45%	51%	49%

Expenses do not include Dr. Kent's salary, interest, depreciation, or retirement contributions.

K. Goodwill

Positive goodwill factors include the excellent clinic location and traffic visibility, staff continuity, clinic growth, clinic net income percentage, and the willingness of Dr. Kent to assist in the changeover and to sign a non-compete covenant.

From a negative standpoint, the physical appearance of the clinic needs to be upgraded.

Based upon the above factors, the goodwill is estimated at five months of average collections for the past twenty-four months, or:

$27,860 per month x 5.00 months = $139,300

APPRAISAL VALUE **$139,300**

VI. FURNITURE, EQUIPMENT, INSTRUMENTS AND SUPPLIES

See attached inventory list.

APPRAISAL VALUE **$39,320**

VII. ACCOUNTS RECEIVABLE

Accounts receivable were $73,000. An aging analysis was not available. The practice appears to be well-managed from a receivables standpoint, since accounts receivable are less than three months of production.

APPRAISAL VALUE *Not Appraised*

VIII. TOTAL PRACTICE APPRAISAL

Facility	*Not Appraised*
Equipment/Supplies	$ 39,320
Goodwill	$139,300
Accounts Receivable	*Not Appraised*
TOTAL	$178,620

B

BUYER AND SELLER WARRANTIES

Provided below are samples of both a seller's and a buyer's warranty from a sample contract of sale. This language is provided as an example and should not be used without advice of counsel.

The information is from an article by Randall K. Berning, J.D., in the August 1987 edition of DENTISTRY TODAY.

SELLER'S WARRANTIES AND REPRESENTATION

A. SELLER warrants that the property being transferred hereunder will be free and clear of any and all liens and encumbrances in his name on the possession date.

B. SELLER further warrants that SELLER does not have any contingent liabilities, or causes of action pending or threatened against SELLER, known and unknown, for any act performed by SELLER or on SELLER's behalf.

(Items A and B provide that the buyer will, in fact, take the practice free and clear with no contingent liablility. This language is very strong. It offers great protection to the buyer because it includes all actions, even those "pending or threatened" "known and unknown.")

C. SELLER hereby agrees to indemnify and hold harmless BUYER from and against such liabilities, lawsuits, or causes of action, including reasonable attorney's fees and court costs.

(Item C has real value for the buyer because the seller is willing to state that he or she is so sure that there will be no pending actions that he or she will pay to protect the buyer from any lawsuits or attorney's fees. Now, many sellers have said, "Why should I be so generous?" The answer is that the buyer must be comfortable with the sale or he or she won't buy, and if a seller cannot say those things, then he or she had better inform the buyer of any pending or threatened actions.)

D. SELLER further warrants that from the date of execution of this agreement and until the date of sale of the practice, he will devote the same portion of his professional time as he has in the past to the operation of the practice.

(Item D is born from experience. It provides that the seller will give "the same portion of time" to the practice until the date of sale as he or she has in the past. Here is what has happened in some instances and why the provision is placed here. A seller, once the deal is closed, may start taking off time or not book as heavily or, in more than one instance, not keep the recall program as tight as he once did.)

E. SELLER further warrants the validity of the facts and figures provided by SELLER to BUYER as true and correct.

F. In that regard, it is the express representation of the SELLER that said amounts of gross receipts, costs, and all proper facts provided are complete.

G. This is not to guarantee the future, but only to specifically warrant as true and complete all past records of SELLER as material fact.

(Items E, F, and G are all related. They serve a dual purpose. First, they are intended to alert the buyer that the facts regarding gross and net are real. The buyer can rely on them. But, they are not the equivalent of facts for the purposes of a projection. Many buyers take over a practice assuming they will be able to produce at or even above the previous doctor. When it does not happen, or it takes a long time to develop, they are disgruntled and bitter. This very valuable provision puts the buyer on notice that while the numbers are real, he should be careful in weighing the future solely on the gross production or net achieved by the former doctor.

Second, the provision can be an important reminder for the seller to avoid loose talk in discussions with a potential buyer. For example, the buyer may come to rely on the seller's early comments that the practice "does around $40,000" per month when in fact it is often at $35–38,000 and only occasionally has hit $40,000. This can create a serious misconception on the part of the buyer, and some sellers who created the misconception early find it embarrassing to straighten out the story when the real facts are presented in the form of tax forms. Far better to be direct and very specific from the beginning of the discussions with the prospective buyer.)

BUYER'S WARRANTIES AND REPRESENTATION

A. BUYER warrants and covenants to SELLER that BUYER has inspected and is familiar with the office premises and the physical condition of all furniture, fixtures, and equipment of said practice.

B. BUYER has had every opportunity to investigate and has investigated the books, records, and financial information.

(Items A and B are related. They place a very heavy burden on the buyer to inspect everything about the practice—physical condition, equipment, and financial aspects. The language "has had every opportunity to investigate and has investigated" is placed for one very important reason: so that the buyer cannot come back to the seller after the sale and complain that he or she did not know what was being purchased. It stops that argument cold.)

C. BUYER has made verification of such data to BUYER's complete satisfaction, and the BUYER is purchasing said practice voluntarily based on BUYER's own judgment and evaluation.

(In item C the buyer is placed on notice by the seller that all items relating to the physical condition, equipment and financial aspects are being agreed to because he or she has made "verification." Again, this is very strong language that will protect the seller in the event the buyer complains after the sale that he did not know or was not told relevant facts. This, of course, does not prevent the buyer from claiming fraud if some fact was misrepresented.)

D. Other than SELLER's warranty, BUYER does not rely upon any verbal or written representation of the SELLER's agent regarding said practice.

(Item D is the provision to remind the buyer that sometimes a sales agent for the practice may misrepresent a part of the physical condition, equipment or financial aspects. But in this provision, the buyer is on notice that he specifically cannot rely on what has been stated by the agent—only the seller. This provision is also important because the buyer, once he has accepted this language, cannot sue the agent for misrepresenting the sale because the buyer states that he or she did not rely solely on the representations as the basis for the sale.)

E. BUYER warrants that however long BUYER utlilizes SELLER's name in connection with said practice, BUYER shall indemnify and hold harmless SELLER from any and all liabilities, and defend against losses, expenses, damages, acts or failure to act, attorney's fees, and court costs that may arise subsequent to the date of sale as the result of the use of SELLER's name. Additionally, BUYER shall have SELLER's name on his malpractice insurance as an added insured party while BUYER uses SELLER's name in connection with said practice.

(Item E is an interesting one. When most sellers prepare the warranties, this item is not covered. Here, the seller definitely does not want his name used. If it is, he wants to be protected. It is a provision worth considering if the seller is going to retire and move out of the area and wants the buyer only to use the seller's name for limited purposes.)

C

REFFERENCES AND SOURCES OF ADDITIONAL INFORMATION

AMA Center for Health Policy Research: The Demographics of physician supply: Trends and projections. Chicago, 1987.

American Medical Association: A physician's guide to gearing up for retirement. Chicago, 1983.

A-dec, Inc.: What to look for when buying dental equipment. Newberg, Oregon, 1985.

Bazerman, Max H.: Why negotiations go wrong. *Psychology Today.* June, 1986.

Berning, Randall K., J.D.: Ideas for shielding your money during transition. *DENTISTRY TODAY.* August, 1987.

Determining the value of your practice: A realistic approach. *JADA.* September, 1984.

Fussell, Paul: Class. New York, Ballantine Books, 1983.

Goldstein, Arnold S.: The Complete Guide to Buying and Selling a Business. New York, Menton, 1986.

Jackson, James B., D.D.S., C.F.P., and Hill, Roger K., M.B.A., A.S.A.: New Trends in Dental Practice Valuation and Associateship Arrangements. Chicago, Quintessence Publishing Co., 1987.

McCormack, Mark H.: The terrible truth about lawyers. *SUCCESS*, November, 1987.

Perkinson, Baxter W. Jr., D.D.S.,: Choosing an associate: How to find your best match. *Dental Management*, December, 1984.

Practice assets: They're too valuable to guess at. *Medical Economics*, October 28, 1984.

Roman, Mark B.: Gold rush. *SUCCESS*, November, 1987.

Schaub, Gary R.: Marketing: For Practice Growth. Portland, *HELP Publications*, 1985.

Schulman, Martin L.: Medical Partnerships & Practice Disposition. New York, Praeger, 1983.

Steiner, Julian, D.D.S., J.D.: Practicing with another dentist: Avoid these legal traps. *Dental Management*, August, 1985.

Sweeney, Dorothy R. and Strogen, Edward M. Jr.: Goodwill: What's it really worth? *Dental Management*, December, 1985.

ABOUT
THE AUTHOR

Gary Schaub has been involved with health care management for the past sixteen years. His company provides practice management consulting and appraisal services for medical and dental offices. He has been responsible for the appraisal and/or sale of over $25,000,000 worth of practices.

His educational background includes a Masters in Business Administration with a major in marketing. He is a Clinical Instructor in Practice Management at the Oregon Health Sciences University. He gives national talks and seminars and has written several practice management publications, including the book Marketing: For Practice Growth.

The author can be reached at Suite V-225, 333 South State Street, Lake Oswego, Oregon 97034. Telephone (503) 697-3502.

DATE DUE

JUN 5 1990			
ILL to BLL			
Due 7-9-91			
JUL 1 0 2001			
DEC 2 6 2007			